Write To Woof 2017

Edited By Robert McCrandall

All rights reserved. All characters appearing in this work are fictitious. Any resemblance to real persons, living or dead is purely coincidental.

No part of this publication may be reproduced, distributed, or transmitted in any form or by any means, including photocopying, recording, or other electronic or mechanical methods, either now known or unknown, without the written permission of the publisher, except in the case of brief quotations embodied in critical reviews and certain other noncommercial uses permitted by copyright law. For permission requests, write to the publisher, "Attention: Permissions Coordinator", at the address below.

Grey Wolfe Publishing, LLC
145 East Fourteen Mile Road
Clawson, Michigan 48017
www.GreyWolfePublishing.com

© 2017 Grey Wolfe Publishing, LLC
Published by Grey Wolfe Publishing, LLC
www.GreyWolfePublishing.com
All Rights Reserved

Print edition ISBN: 978-1628281873
E-Book edition ISBN: 978-1628281880
Library of Congress Control Number: 2017941680

Write To Woof 2017

Edited By Robert McCrandall

Dedication

Write To Woof is an annual anthology published by Grey Wolfe Publishing. The goal of this year's collection is to bring awareness to the roles dogs play in our lives... as companions, helpers and teachers. Whether pure-bred or rescued Mutt; each enhances our lives like no other creature on earth.

This book is lovingly dedicated to Finnigan, the newest member of our Grey Wolfe Pack. His photo appears on the cover and on the Contributing Author Page. At almost two years old, he is a tremendous companion, full of life and love.

Acknowledgements

We would like to send out a special Thank You to the authors who submitted their work for this book. It is because of your dedication to dogs, as well as the writing craft, that we have been able to produce such a spectacular tribute to our furry friends!

We also want to thank the good people of Wolf Haven International who work tirelessly day after day to make sure that displaced wolves from all over the country can live out the remainder of their lives in peace and comfort.

And finally, we want to thank you, the person who purchased this book and are about to read it. Because of your interest in dogs, or perhaps because of the relationship you have with one of the authors, dogs with particular challenges will be partnered with extraordinary families as they grow to trust again... feel safe again... love again... forever.

Table of Contents

Beloved Buster	Kimberly Wisener	1
A Triolet	Mark Hudson	4
Christmas with the Dogs	Mark Hudson	5
Daisy for One Day	Mark Hudson	7
Daisy the Pizza Eating Dog	Mark Hudson	10
Dogs – Comforters and Protectors	Mark Hudson	11
Dogstar Date: June, Friday the 13th, 1997	Bobbie Growth	13
Fair Exchange	Larry Lefkowitz	19
Five Dog Kaikus	A.J. Juffman	24
Gabriel the Guide Dog	Jon Moray	25
Hanover's Adversities	R. Bremner	29
I Love My Pups	Lisa Scuderi-Burkimsher	41
Keith's Dog	Mark Hudson	43

Lady	R. Bremner	44
Longing for Your True home	Mark Hudson	52
Lucky	Christopher Woods	55
McKenzie	Carol S. Hanson	58
Mighty Levi	Mark Hudson	62
New Lessons	Larry Lefkowitz	64
Spice	R. Bremner	67
Sugar: Saying Goodbye	Audra Coleman	75
Taking Care of Levi Part Two	Mark Hudson	79
The Guard's Dog	R. Bremner	80
The Little Old Man and Pepi	Madelyn Kamen	90
Walter	Margaret Peterson	93
When She Goes	Jessica Rigby	95
Who Is In Charge?	Mark Hudson	96

Contributing Authors — **97**

Beloved Buster
Kimberly Wisener

Flora was busy in the kitchen, peeling a potato when she heard a funny noise. It is the early seventies, and with no air conditioning, the back door is open to let in a little breeze. She continues to hear the noise and puts down the peeler to step toward the back door that accesses the garage. She looks out but doesn't step out yet.

Buster, the most fabulous dog in the world, is busy. She watches as he comes into the garage and goes towards his chair— yes, he has his own chair! He is holding something in his mouth. Flora bends closer to the door and realizes it is a baby chick. Buster stops next to a box by his chair and deposits the chick on top. The top of the box is folded over, and he pushes down with his nose, and the chick goes in. The top of the box closes back. It sounds like there are several already in the box. He walks back out of the garage toward the neighbor's yard, probably to get another.

Flora quickly ties the belt to her bathrobe and steps out. She takes the box and opens it to find three small chicks. She is flabbergasted. This is not the first gift Buster has brought home. The list is long, including bunnies. He has a very soft mouth and never hurts any of the treasures he delivers. The neighbors are new and have a few chickens, but probably don't know they are missing some chicks.

Flora walks next door and sees Buster near a big chicken and calls for him to go home. She scolds him as she is knocking on the neighbor's door to return the chicks. Buster left the chicks alone after that, and would only chase them out of the yard.

He was always so smart and out for an adventure. He would wait at the end of the road for Flora's husband to come home each day, race him to the house and cheat just a bit so he could be waiting when Ed stepped out of the truck. It was amazing that he knew just the time to get there. He would grin for a cookie. He would chase her sons across the yard and through their pup tent until he got tired and sat on top of the tent, trapping them inside to stop them from running. He loved Flora's sons and her husband, but he only brought gifts to her.

One time, Flora brought home a kitten. Buster quickly adopted the kitten and let it sleep with him on his chair. He thought the kitten belonged to him. If the kitten got into trouble doing something he shouldn't be doing, Buster was there, picking him up and taking him back to their chair.

Buster was an Airedale/German shepherd mix. He was a medium sized dog, buff colored and black. He loved to share ice cream cones with the boys. He would take a lick, and the boys would take a lick. He was very protective of the boys. They could not go anywhere without him. He would wrestle with them and chew on the cuffs of their pants. He was their best friend. When the gate to the house was shut by Ed for the night, no one would dare come into the yard because Buster was in protection mode.

At times, the house would flood during a tropical storm. Buster did not like to come in the house. Flora made him come in, and he would move farther in the house as the water moved toward him. She had him up on the bed, and he was so afraid to move because he knew he really wasn't supposed to be there.

The family knew that Buster's chair was Buster's chair, but when guests came over, they sometimes had to figure it out. The boys had a friend that visited and sat in Buster's chair. Buster proceeded to stare the kid down until he finally moved.

Buster would be referred to as just a "good old dog" by the family. He lived to be thirteen years old and died in his sleep. The youngest boy stayed home from school the morning Buster didn't wake up and buried him. He was thirteen, too, and had grown up every day of his life with Buster. There would be other pets, but none that compared to their beloved Buster.

A Triolet
Mark Hudson

Source: The Spokesman Review January 18, 2017
Chocolate is not for Canines by Stephanie Petite

There was a man who had a dog named Ellie;
and for Christmas he had a big chocolate fish.
And the dog ate the fish that filled his belly.
There was a man who had a dog named Ellie,
The dog ate what shouldn't be on his dish.
The fact the dog survived was the Christmas wish;
There once was a man, who had a dog named Ellie,
and the dog ate the fish that filled his belly.

Christmas with the Dogs
Mark Hudson

I spent Christmas with my sister, who dog sits for a job. Her kids, my niece and nephew, already have a dog named Spot. My sister was dog-sitting two elderly retrievers, Grace and Will.

As I sit here writing my notes on this article, I am covered head to toe in dog hair! I will simply have to throw my clothes in the laundry when I get home.

I ate dinner with my niece and nephew, and then they raced back down to the basement to play the new video games my nephew got for Christmas. They didn't poke their head up again until it was time for presents and desert. Then after that, they disappeared again.

But the two dogs, Will and Grace, showed loyalty and love to me, as if I wasn't a stranger in their house! They constantly approached me to be petted, and loved the attention.

At one point my sister stepped out, and I played with the dogs for twenty minutes. Then when I went to bed in the living room, Will, the oldest dog, insisted on sleeping at my feet, and if I woke up, he would offer his head to pet!

There are many pros and cons to owning a dog. For instance, I live in the Chicago-land area, and I live right next to Lake Michigan. There are days that it is unbearably cold. Yet, I see dog owners walking their dogs at all hours of the night in a frozen tundra, and only a true dog lover would do that!

I see why owning a dog can be both rewarding and challenging. Is it worth it to have a dog, with all the chores you have to do, vacuuming up all the hair, constantly buying pet food, and the vet bills? I look at all the dog lovers in my community, and my sister, and I say, yes, it's worth it!

But taking care of a pet is a commitment, and you shouldn't take it on if you can't handle it.

As I conclude my notes on this story, Grace just came up to the table, looked at me and wagged her tail. I should show the dogs some attention before I go back home. Happy Holidays, everybody!

Daisy for One Day
Mark Hudson

I walked home discouraged. I was so depressed! I was an artist and a writer, and people just didn't understand! I was on the proverbial pity pot in this gloom and doom town. And everybody around me was so depressed. My forty-sixth birthday was coming up, and what did that mean? Cake and ice cream?

Choo-choo trains? I was growing old, and I was bald as an eagle, but without the dignity, nor the cult status. I couldn't fly like an eagle, when I was crawling like an inchworm.

As I entered the elevator, I saw my neighbor, the attorney, who had his dog Daisy. That dog was spoiled by his owner, and everybody in the building.

Why, the people in the building loved that dog more than me! If I only I could be a dog!

I got home and still felt sad! Should I end it all? I took my bottle of Fred Flintstone chewable vitamins and downed the bottle. I prayed I wouldn't wake up, or at least if I did, I'd wake up in a better place.

When I woke up, I was Daisy the Dog! I had somehow been magically transported into my neighbor's apartment, and I was his dog! I was lying on a beanbag, sweating under a heavy air conditioner!

My master was feeding me tons of pizza. I needed to go number two. But I didn't know how to tell this to my master. I was new at this dog thing.

He must've read me like a book. "Oh, you want to go poo-poo, don't you Daisy?" I guess I must've nodded my head, wagged my tail in agreement. Could it be more obvious?

So, my master put a leash on me and put me in the elevator. In the elevator, there was a gorgeous woman in the elevator! She said, "Oh, your dog is so cute!" and petted me on the head, and massaged my ears! Why couldn't that ever happen to me when I was human? All I could do is drool like a fool, and stick my tongue out, panting! It's what I secretly wished to do as a human being, but I couldn't do, my parents taught me manners!

My master brought me out to the front lawn, and I let out a fresh poop to decorate the grass. Suddenly, I didn't feel so cute. A bunch of grade-school kids were laughing, and I felt self-conscious! They better be grateful they're not a dog! Their parents better monitor how many Fred Flintstone vitamins they take, or they might be the next one to be a dog!

Then, my master took me inside, and put me in a cage and said, "Good night."

"Good night?" It was dark and uncomfortable! Ouch! What was this? Oh, if only I could only be a human again, I'll never complain again! I begin to think like Dorothy from Wizard of Oz.

There's no place like home...

Then a weird thing happened. I found myself in my own bed, in my own apartment, and Daisy was at my side, licking my face.

"Yuck!" I said.

Then, Daisy disappeared. Everything was back to normal. What happened?

I checked my wastebasket and there were no bottles of vitamins that I took. Then I found it. A can of bad tomatoes must've given me the bad hallucinations, and guess what had also been mixed into it, dog food! I smelled a lawsuit on my hands! So, I consulted the very same neighbor, the attorney, and he helped me sue Happy Foods where I got the tomatoes. Needless to say, they were not too happy. I won the case, I had a million dollars and I bought a mansion in Lake Forest, and I became like Howard Hughes, and bought an anorexic poodle who refused to eat.

When he peed on my thousand-dollar rug, that was the last straw. I threw him out on the street, and then ten minutes later I cried, and packed all my belongings in a bag and a stick, and took off to find my dog looking like Charlie Chaplin, or a tramp, or something.

We got to about Rogers park with all the bull dogs and killer canines, and we got scared, and we both ran back home, where we eat tons of pizza, and my philosophy is, "Don't read newspapers, it's too depressing.

Put them on your rug, so your dog can pee on it." I may be nothing but a "hound dog" but at least I wasn't Elvis Presley. Every dog has his day.

Daisy the Pizza Eating Dog
Mark Hudson

I have a neighbor in my apartment building who has a wonderful dog named Daisy, who makes people all around the building happy.

Last night, I saw my neighbor in the elevator, and he had just got a pizza from a delivery guy.

I said, "Wow, you're going to have a good dinner tonight!"

And he said, "Well part of it is for me, and part of it is for my dog. I tried Daisy's dog food, but what she really needs is pizza."

I said, "You mean you ate dog food?"

It was just a misunderstanding, because I was really tired. I thought he meant he ate some of his dog's food! But what he really meant was he tried different dog foods for Daisy, and found out what served the dog best was scraps from pizza! Boy, some creatures live like royalty!

Sometimes, I wish I was a dog!

Dogs—
Comforters and Protectors
Mark Hudson

I have a volunteer job at my church where I work with the kids. Every Sunday, I check the kids into Sunday School. They never cease to cheer me up.

Today, the Sunday School teacher was sitting down drawing with the kids, and one boy said, "I hate dogs."

The teacher was like, "What? Why?"

"Because my sister and I were on a trip to Ethiopia and there were these mean dogs guarding the house, and they scared us," the boy replied.

The teacher said, "Well, they were just doing their job! They were protecting their house because they loved their master! When I was a kid, I had a dog, and I would tell my dog all my problems, and it would lick away my tears."

I remembered being a kid, and I had a babysitter over, and they said, "If you hear any funny noises, call the police."

And my babysitter must've let me watch a scary movie, because I was trying to sleep, and I heard the rustling of leaves, so I told the babysitter, "I think someone is out there." So we called the police, and I remember my dog barking like crazy at the cops, being a good guard dog, and me in my pajamas as cops walking around with flashlights. That was the seventies. Nowadays, I don't know what emergency it would take to get the cops out.

Just missing my childhood dog, and remembering how she was the sweetest member of our family. You can learn how to treat people by having a dog.

DOGSTAR DATE:
June, Friday the 13th, 1997
Bobbie Groth

Today? Our annual trip to the vet for doggie shots. They are both senile. BJ, a black and tan mini Australian Shepherd can't see, hear, or smell (even though she DOES stink). She barks wildly every once in a while, when she remembers she's a dog, though.

BJ has been a veritable Houdini ever since we got her—she can open every door in the house and get out of any dog pen or crate ever designed. Twelve-foot fencing is no object to her—she climbs right up and over it. That's why we have the only dog pen in town with *roof* fencing. BJ is a rescue who came to us with heartworms, so she was no bargain.

Shadow, our Lab-Pointer mix, is also a rescue. Clearly, I'm a slow learner. His former owner enjoyed picking him up by his ears and tossing him down the stairs. It took hours and hours of offering delectable treats to finally teach him how to go up to our second floor and down again without being carried.

He still won't do it *all* by himself. In the middle of the night, he goes and stands at the top of the stairs and begins to moan and whine. It finally reaches such a pitch that the kids are disturbed from their sleep. Muzzy voices begin to plead in the dark:

"Shadow, go to sleep."

"Shadow! Be quiet!"

"Shadow, just go by yourself!"

"Shadow, noooooooo...."

Finally, one of them breaks. He or she gets out of bed, turns on the hall light, shuffles to the stairs, and mumbles sleepy encouragement while Shadow maneuvers the steps. You see, Shadow doesn't need anyone to *help* him down, he just wants someone to *watch*.

Shadow is now gray around the muzzle, but he has a huge deep bark, is still puppy-hyperactive, and can't stand being separated from BJ. If that happens, he whines and howls until they are reunited—sounds like he's got his tail caught in a trash compactor. (I, for one, wonder if BJ even knows he's there). Kinda reminds me of that old ditty sung to "The Irish Washerwoman." *Oh, MacTavish is dead, and his brother don't know it, his brother is dead, and MacTavish don't know it. Each of them died in the very same bed, and neither one knows that the other is dead.*

Any reasonable person can understand why going for our annual checkup with the vet is not something I look forward to. Old dogs stink, and our two dogs—one being a shepherd and one being a water dog—stink a lot. So, I instructed the kids to bathe them yesterday and then to bathe them again today so that we could all be in the examining room together without passing out.

Yesterday they got a dandy bath, but the kids did not come home from school and bathe them again today ("We did that yesterday!"). So, I get home and have to run them through a quickie shampoo. With only twenty minutes until our appointment, there is insufficient dry time before we all get in the car together. That means we no doubt will all get out smelling like wet dog.

Did I say I'm allergic to dogs too? So, I had to make the two girls come along and hold the dogs so they won't touch me, and little Mike has to be with us since he's too young to leave at home alone.

Gabe, the official "owner" of Shadow and the oldest and strongest of our brood, somehow manages to go MIA for this expedition even though I clearly remember a long heartfelt letter from him when he was begging to get the dog. It said, "I will take care of him so well you will never even know we have a dog." Believe me, I know we have a dog. I put a blanket over my car seats so the pooches won't touch those either.

It's only a matter of a few blocks drive to the vet, but it's a lot safer to have everyone contained in the car. I don't want any escapees. When we get there, there's the usual scramble as BJ and Shadow leap from the car tearing their leashes out of the hands of their young "owners." After a bit of whoopee-ti-yi-yo, they are rounded up.

Then we have to drag them, literally drag them by the collar, through the front door. They have taken one little doggie sniff and know immediately where they are.

No amount of cajoling on the part of the vet assistant can persuade them to sit on the scale and get weighed. Oh no, they fling themselves around in circles. Let the record reflect that according to the little digital screen on the scale, Shadow weighs somewhere between five and fifty-five pounds and BJ's somewhere between eighteen and thirty pounds. I think her more advanced age and arthritis makes her a little slower than he is.

Finally, it's time for us to go into the examining room. Repeat the scene where dogs get dragged forcefully by their human, toenails scrabbling madly on the floor trying to gain purchase to escape while the children attempt to push them through the door from behind.

In there. We are actually all in the examining room and are waiting for the vet. The two girls are paying meticulous attention to the posters featuring various parts of a dog's insides. They make vomiting noises to torture their little brother.

Suddenly, a four-foot stream of doggie effluvia erupts from BJ's back end, spraying the floor and fully painting Mike's little shoe. He starts to cry as his two sisters laugh hysterically at him.

I limp out to the front desk gagging and trying to hold my nose, with the offending dog in tow. I tell them she "gets a little too excited" and that for the wellbeing of all I'm going to take her outside and tie her to the railing. I invite the vet to examine her out there, given her now intensified less-than-clean condition. I leave Mikey outside with her since his shoe is in as miserable shape as she is. I go back inside.

They immediately move us to another examining room until the Terminator can be found to incinerate the first one. Now remember, BJ has disappeared from the scene. Three, two, one: Shadow goes psycho. He begins to jump around and roll his eyes, trying to bite everyone in sight. The two girls plaster themselves against the wall and intelligently refuse to go any closer to him.

The vet just can't seem to get him up on the examining table. Shadow won't let anyone touch him or lift him—his eyes just start going in circles and his teeth commence snapping. The good doctor then tries to get two different kinds of muzzles on him, which also proves impossible. The dog is, after all, not stupid.

Finally, the vet sets his jaw and tells me to take Shadow home. He gives me a bottle of tranquilizers and commands that I "experiment" with "the dog" to find out how many it takes to sedate him and how long the stupor will last.

Only when I am armed with this information may I make an appointment and bring him back—and then only if Shadow is comatose and already muzzled. I can't believe we'll have to go through a day like this again.

I leave the girls in the exam room with Shadow, and the vet and I go out to where BJ is still tethered to the railing. Mike is leaned against it next to BJ, his left foot and one partially browned sneaker extended as far away from his nose as he can manage.

I tell the vet that BJ is blind, deaf, and can't smell. He feels all over her poor little old doggie body. He must've forgotten why we were having this much fun out in the parking lot because he reaches right up into the fur of her back end, then pulls his hand out shaking it vigorously. I notice he doesn't use it for anything else again. But we do have a half victory: BJ actually gets her shots.

The trip home is the next challenge. I am NOT allowing BJ back in the car with her dysentery-dripping nine-inch-long hind leg hair. Since Mike is the one with the un-tastefully painted shoe that I don't want in the car either, I make him walk her home on her leash. I follow closely in the car, driving right up against the curb behind them like a perv.

The girls, of course, are still paralyzed with mirth at their little brother's misfortune, and Mikey. Is. Still. Crying. Did he ever stop bawling through this whole hellish outing? I am some kind of bad mother that I don't even know.

Shadow, meanwhile, sees that BJ is not in the car and begins whining and howling, ramping it up until it's at a deafening pitch and the girls' jollity has turned to angry bellowing at me to make him stop. Seriously, who are they kidding?

All this and then there is more, for it is not the end of this lovely evening. I need to spray down BJ's back end and Mike's shoe before they go into the house, and this necessitates the two girls holding the dogs while I first enter our humble abode by myself to find some appropriate soap.

To my surprise, I cannot get my key into the back door lock. So, as my husband arrives home from work happily waving at our little domestic gathering and our eldest nonchalantly saunters up the driveway dribbling a basketball, the rest of us are standing around the back door, two of our members dripping um—poop—two of our members being unhelpfully obnoxious, and one of us blathering at full volume about the back door lock being broken and "Who shoved spaghetti into it?!"

Anybody want to buy some kids and dogs? Cheap? Please don't walk away! I'll come down on my price! I'll come down further! I'll pay *YOU* to take them away!

Fair Exchange
Larry Lefkowitz

The downstairs neighbor was peeved at me once again. This time because I had committed the sin of allowing a plate of steaks, which I had finished barbecuing and left to cool on the balcony railing, to fall onto the grass of his ground floor apartment, narrowly missing his beloved dog, a floor-mop-looking creature of Japanese pedigree. I apologized and he accepted my tendered regrets with the miffed, if paranoid, rejoinder, "Don't enter into my life and I won't enter into yours."

I mumbled to myself, "Who would want to enter into your life?" A life which centered around the dog and my neighbor's ecological bent – preparing mulch in fall and spreading it in spring (or was it vice-versa?), filling his car's tank with all sorts of home-made fuels, for all I know made from the mulch, constantly tinkering with a would-be solar providing apparatus of his own design, and otherwise tailoring his life as if he wanted to garner the *In Tune with Nature* award of the year from Al Gore.

The moment I asked, or commented, the words last quoted, I was overcome by a strange feeling – a kind of numbed loss of consciousness followed by my seeing myself—my new self (me-in-my-neighbor) looking up at my old self (which I assumed was now him-in-me). I was momentarily stunned – an understandable reaction – especially as I don't care for dogs, or pets of any kind, and suddenly I was suffused with love toward "Toto" (Toto was my neighbor's dog, named in honor of Dorothy's pooch from 'The Wizard of Oz'), who lay near my feet, as sessile as a Japanese rock garden, whose only identifiable activity consisted of barking when his repose was disturbed. The 'near miss' had produced a virtual cacophony of canine protest, which may have stimulated that of his owner.

What had caused this exchange of—what—personalities, souls? I could not comprehend. True, a lightning bolt had shattered the otherwise blue sky at almost the same time, but I hardly thought such summer lightning capable of...

Could it be my disparaging words towards my neighbor's life had brought about the exact opposite of the question posed? Some kind of punishment imposed upon me for my hubris, prideful, statement. Or was I being punished for not liking dogs? Surely, I told myself, fate didn't move on four legs, and yet maybe the Japanese creature had put a Zen curse on me?

It was true that for the first time I thought that Reginald, my neighbor, possessed some redeeming features and that Tony – me, or the former me – had some negative personality aspects that had escaped my awareness or my attention previous to the transformation. But still, I preferred being Tony and not Reginald.

Suddenly my posing of questions gave way to fright. What if Reginald preferred being Tony and it was he who was somehow responsible for the transformation (who knew what was in his mulch?—at the same time I felt an appreciation of the mulch) and who had no intention of changing back. Well, I could always take comfort in Toto, whom I indeed now felt very close to. But to be Reginald – no, too many aspects of his personality rubbed me – still – the wrong way or, perhaps mindful of my own aspects – my former ones, I hadn't adjusted fully to the change.

Tony, standing on the balcony, looked like a mirror image of my previous corporeal self, except that, in contrast to my usually smug expression, his expression was one of bemusement. It seemed he, too, was groping to comprehend the fact of the exchange.

Both of us were speechless.

For a time.

"Be sure to take good care of the dog," he admonished me, proof that he had indeed grasped the significance of what had happened, though his tone was one of not caring, or even irony, a tone I recognized as (formerly) mine. And he always had called the dog "Toto". Yup, he was me, all right.

"Of course, I will," I agreed," Toto is a wonderful companion to me." I couldn't believe I had said this.

Carelessly leaning on the balcony railing, hands in his pockets, his expression one of mild disdain, hardly deigning to look at me, he said, "Tony, I confess I always thought you something of a dolt, but now I see that you were, if somewhat fustian, a rough diamond."

"And I was wrong about you, too, Reginald (I had always called him to his face, "Reggie", since I knew he didn't like the nickname). You are what the world needs in these ecological testing-times." I was dead serious, not a trace of mockery.

"Still," he said in a kind of whining tone (that was still Reginald), I'd like to be returned to my former self. No offense, Tony (he had always called me 'Anthony' since he knew I preferred 'Tony'). I kind of miss the mop – that is, Toto."

"And I miss dumping my food on him," I said against my will. It seems 'the change' hadn't wiped out all former feelings, which Freud no doubt would claim were too dominant to be transformed.

"So, what do we do about it? "I asked.

"Turn around three times and make a wish," said Tony, or rather Reginald that remained in him, for the words were not mocking but serious in tone.

I stared to laugh, remembering that Reginald was into

Children's Media, fantasy department, and had even published a kind of concordance of the Hobbits books, but the now Reginald in me stifled both the laughter and the doubt, and even caused me to regard it as a good idea. "Do you think it will work?"

"It worked for Dorothy in T*he Wizard of Oz*. Or maybe it was Snow White or The Little Prince… I don't remember, but it worked for them, or one of them. Yes, it will work," insisted Tony-Reginald. "We have to do it together, I feel. A kind of positive synergism."

Reginald-Tony nodded, convinced against my better, or former, instincts.

"One, two, three—now" said Tony-Reginald.

He, Tony-Reginald and I, Reginald-Tony, turned around three times and wished ourselves our former selves.

Positive synergism or negative magnetism or magical realism, or whatever: it worked.

"Whew," said Tony reborn.

"Thank heavens," said Reginald resurrected.

"How'd you like a steak, Reginald old boy?" Tony heard himself ask, to his surprise.

"Don't mind if I do," replied Reginald.

"I'll put one on for the dog – for Toto, too"

"Toto would appreciate it. I'll even contribute my own substitute for charcoal—global warming, you know."

"Alright, Reginald, I just hope it won't affect the taste."

"Taste is a matter of conscience," said Reginald.

I was about to pour scorn on this, but held back. I didn't want to risk another transformation – even though the sky was as blue as that above Kansas before the twister descended on Dorothy out of a clear blue sky.

Five Dog Haikus
A.J. Huffman

I am Chihuahua.
My tiny voice speaks volumes
from tea cup or purse.

I am Doberman.
Sleek black, protection machine.
Love is my command.

I am Labrador.
I love to play.   Throw the ball.
I always retrieve.

I am Pekinese.
Long-haired, flat-faced lap warmer.
Queen of every couch.

I am Rottweiler.
Household security.
I do more than drool.

Gabriel the Guide Dog
Jon Moray

Michael nervously surveyed his wristwatch while sandwiched inside an over-crowded city bus. It was his means of commuting to his place of employment, doing tech support for a large banking firm. The stench of collective morning perspiration compounded his fidgety anxiety as he violently pulled on the cord to alert the driver he would exit at the next stop. Before the bus came to a full stop, Michael began pushing past people to get to the side exit, amid colorful, choice words from the perturbed victims.

"Sorry, I am behind schedule," was his empty apology, as he jumped off of the bottom step of the bus. Behind schedule for Michael, meant thirty seconds to one minute lost off his calculated life. He was actually two city blocks from his job and had forty-five minutes to get there, short of taking a pit stop to purchase his morning bagel at the bakery.

He made a dash for the intersection to cross the street as if a football was in his hands and a Super Bowl victory was hanging in the balance. He huffed at the realization he would have to lose a few more seconds; really making him late for an extra early arrival at work.

He and a crowd of other pedestrians waited under a toasty sun as a blur of cars screamed by. While stomping his feet in a fury of impatient theatrics, he noticed a blind man accompanied by a guide dog wearing a bright red identification vest, standing beside him. The flurry of cars vanished, and the crowd began to cross the street against the green light.

Michael rushed across and made a right at the sidewalk, but also noticed the man and the dog still waiting for the light to change. With curiosity peaked, he slowed his motion enough to see the man and dog cross with the signal change. His demeanor warmed momentarily as he jolted into the bakery.

If the bus running late didn't cause a five-alarm fire in his head, the line of seven customers ahead of him should, as he cussed under his breath.

An elevated heartbeat and a constant peak at his watch dominated his emotions until the man and dog approached from behind.

Michal looked back with a smile at the Labrador Retriever, who was looking up at him with a tilted head, temporarily distorting the triangle flap that covered his ears.

"That is quite a dog you have there. Very disciplined. It wouldn't move until the light turned green."

The man adjusted his black shaded glasses and nodded. "Yes, he is very disciplined, very loyal, and very loving. I trust him with my life, as you can see."

The chocolate colored dog, with a smooth, shiny coat, began investigating Michael with his nose, sniffing in the scent of his loafers and up to the knee of his Dockers slacks.

"Gabriel seems to like you," smiled the blind man.

"Gabriel?"

"Yes, my dog's name is Gabriel. If he sniffs you, he likes you, and he has been sniffing you non-stop."

Michael returned the amicable gesture by gently petting Gabriel's head.

"He likes to be scratched behind the ears," the man added.

Michael obliged hurriedly while noticing he was now next in line.

Suddenly, Gabriel shook uncontrollably for a moment.

"Yes, Gabriel, I can feel it too," commented the man. "Gabriel has noticed you to be quite impatient, Sir. His shaking alerted me to it."

"He's got me pegged, alright. Gabriel is also very smart." Michael placed his order, toasted sesame seed bagel with extra cream cheese. The man ordered a plain bagel with nothing on it.

The welcoming aroma of fresh baked bread rendered the blind man with inhaled-filled satisfaction, in vast contrast to Michael's lip biting ignorance of his sense of smell.

The blind man received his order first, to Michael's dismay, mentally calculating time wasted.

"Have a good day, Sir," cheered the man, as he and Gabriel headed for the exit. Michael received his order shortly thereafter and scurried out the store.

Michael dashed past the man and the dog while trying to make the light that was now turning yellow. Just as the light turned red, Gabriel barked loudly, and his powerful alert stopped Michael in his tracks as a vehicle raced by in his projected path.

Michael gulped audibly and staggered towards a lamppost to break his fall as the thought of what might've happened left his legs quivering under him.

"Are you okay?" asked the blind man.

Michael took a few moments to gather himself as Gabriel began licking the back of his hand. "I am okay now. Your dog might've just saved my life," Gabriel gasped.

"That's why it is very easy for me to trust him with my life."

Michael smiled and gripped the man's hand. "Perhaps, I should slow down. I don't have a dog to save my butt when I hurry out of control." Michael bent down to scrub the back of Gabriel's ears while rubbing his nose against the dog's.

"I wish for you and your loyal companion to have a great day. I hope we meet again," beamed Michael.

The blind man returned the sentiment, Gabriel stood focusing on the signal, and the trio waited patiently for the light to change.

Hanover's Adversities
R. Bremner

Hanover has always been a hard-luck dog. It's like the stars have situated themselves in the worst possible alignment for him. Even back to the day he came into our lives, he was a dog of woe. I remember picking him up from the shelter. A skinny, spindly cocker spaniel full of bounce. Though we already had a dog, my wife let herself be talked into fostering Hanover for a day or two, "until a good home could be found for him". Or perhaps, more likely, my wife asked for the chance to foster him.

On the drive from the animal shelter to the house, this energetic creature bounced all around the car, most frequently landing in my lap. No matter how often I pushed him off, the nervous creature always wound up there again.

At the house, he seemed to make himself right at home. He gobbled up the food we set out for him and bounded through the house, jumping on chairs and beds alike. Our regular dog Lady, was a blind cocker spaniel, with a deep voice, and she seemed a bit confused by Hanover's boisterousness.

That night, Hanover tried to jump on our bed when we retired. My wife pushed him off. He jumped up a second time, and my wife pushed him off again. This time, he fell into a suitcase, and was startled into quiet. So, we were all able to sleep.

The next day, Hanover stayed home with my wife and son while I went to work. My wife had taken to calling him "Handsome" instead of Hanover, and he spent most of his time trailing after my son. A five-year-old cannot do much with a blind dog, so Sanjay was happy to have a dog that was active.

I arrived home from work about five-thirty that night, as usual, and opened the front door. I expected to be greeted by my wife and son. Instead, it was Hanover, who bolted out the door and raced around the house, with a laughing Sanjay right behind him. Then he raced back to the front, right into the busy street. I groaned as Hanover ran right into a moving car.

The poor dog was in agony moaning, as he lay on his side. My wife Sharon began dialing 911, but someone in the street had beat us to it, and a police car was right there. Sharon attempted to lift Hanover, but the dog bit her. You couldn't blame him. He was wounded and scared. The policeman lifted Hanover onto a child's round sled I provided.

"He's a good dog," the cop said. "He could have fought me but he didn't. Where you gonna take him?"

"There's a vet we use in the next town. If they're open, we'll go there." The cop helped me slide the sled into the back seat, while Sharon called the vet. I wanted to bring her to an emergency room first, but she wrapped her hand and sat in the back seat with the dog. We had to take Sanjay, as he was too young to be left alone, and somehow, we squeezed his child seat in. We left Lady, our blind cocker home.

"Has Lady gone out after dinner?" I asked.

"No, but she'll hold it. She's a good dog."

The vet took him in immediately. After an examination, he concluded that he would give the dog a painkiller, then set the leg. It might hold, it might not. Hanover would have to stay overnight.

The next day I stopped over after work, bringing Sanjay with me. The vet explained that Hanover's situation was very precarious. I should be very careful, not letting him climb stairs, or go out of the house on his own, and he should be carried until the leg bone was secure in the hip socket.

At home, we treated him gingerly. I lifted him up gently and carried him outside when it was time for him to go. We all watched him carefully.

But despite all our care, the setting did not hold up, and poor Hanover's frame collapsed. We were beside ourselves. We called the shelter from whence he came, and they arranged for treatment at a surgical center. We took the dog there, and were amazed at the complexity of the place. A nurse took him from my arms, and we sat in a waiting room. Then we were led to a room where Hanover sat on the floor and a surgeon explained the treatment to us.

"We'll have to cut the bone where it sticks out of the socket," he said, demonstrating by putting one fist into his other, open hand. "The leg will then be free, with no connection to the hip... but that's okay, he'll be fine. The leg will swing free in the socket... you just have to make sure he gets plenty of exercise."

We were to leave the dog and await their call. The surgery would take place the next day, and he would remain at the hospital several days.

"No sense in coming to see him tomorrow. He'll be doped up through the whole day."

So, we left him. But we called the next day and were told that he was recovering. And we went there anyway. They wouldn't let us into the room where he was recuperating, but they opened the door so we could see. He had a big bandage on his hip and he was sleeping. He seemed to be comfortable, so we left a bit reassured.

We came again the next day to learn that there had been a remarkable recovery. He was walking quite well, though favoring one side, and we could take him home.

"We all love him here," said the nurse. "He's so cute and so stoic."

We got to see the doctor, this time a woman, and thank her. "Give him lots of exercise, otherwise the leg will get tight and calcium deposits will form in the socket, and we'll have to operate again. Long walks and swims are the best for him. Take him to a doggie pool." I had never heard of a doggie pool, but I thanked her and Hanover walked himself to the car. It was almost funny, the exit from the highway to this clinic involved a treacherous turnoff across a busy intersection at which there was next to no visibility. I wondered how many dogs and cats had been injured in accidents on the way to the clinic!

We took Hanover home and he was terrific. He and our blind dog, Lady, became fast friends. The would both run to the door barking whenever there was a noise outside, the blind dog following in Hanover's wake, Hanover soon made himself at home and lorded it over Lady. Once I caught him in the backyard peeing on her head. I quickly pulled him away and gave him a lengthy scolding. He must have understood, because I never saw him try that trick again.

Hanover developed a special relationship with Sanjay. The two were always together. Hanover slept at his feet. Sanjay felt that Hanover was the most intelligent dog who ever lived, and I have to confess I thought he was remarkably smart myself. He knew how to open doors using his paws on the doorknobs, and he always seemed to know what we were thinking.

Sanjay told a friend that Hanover had taught him a "pre-historic dog language" and introduced him to the god of the dogs, Olkmo. They would sit on our front lawn and Sanjay would chant "OLK-MO! OLK-MO!" while Hanover sat by his side. When the awful tragedy of September 11, 2001 occurred, we all felt deeply moved. Sanjay told us that at night while he was sleeping, Hanover would leap into action and go the many miles to New York to search through the rubble and pull out survivors, returning at dawn. I think he truly believed it.

So, the years passed. Lady died, and Hanover was left alone, but he always had Sanjay. As Sanjay grew, he took over the job of walking Hanover, and he would not let anyone else do it. Hanover used to sit by the door until Sanjay returned from school. Sanjay would take Hanover, or "Hansie" as he nicknamed the dog, on all his play sessions with the other kids, and they all came to know and love "Hansie".

As time went on, the boy grew and the dog aged. We started taking Hanover to the dog park on weekends. Although he was small compared to the Boxers, Shepherds, and Labradors there, Hanover would always bully the other dogs and lord it over them. He wouldn't back down from any of them. Though some dogs would challenge him, his fierceness and loud voice would put them in their places.

About this time, we adopted another pup, who was tiny at first but soon grew into a huge strapping fellow with a deep-throated bark. Sharon thought Hanover was getting old now and a puppy would ease Sanjay's pain if Hanover passed away. Justin was a German Shepherd mix with very sharp teeth and claws. However, Hanover had no trouble asserting his dominance over Justin. With his high-pitched barks and a well-placed nip now and again, Hanover showed Justin who was the boss.

Hanover was still pretty feisty and Sanjay was in eighth grade when I took them to the dog park one July fourth. Because of the holiday, the park was nearly deserted. Only one other person was present, on a bench at the far end of the park.

Hanover trotted around, seeming pleased. I lost sight of him for a moment as he disappeared behind the woman's bench. Then I heard this squealing sound, sounding like a dog was in great pain or fear. I ran toward the bench.

There was Hanover, on his back, with two pit bulls on top of him, biting and scratching. I looked around and spied a plastic ball-throwing rod close by. I grabbed the rod and swung it again and again, hitting the pit bulls as hard as I could. For some strange reason, they did not attack me, but left Hanover. Perhaps they were frozen with surprise. Or pain. Or fear.

"Run! Run to the car!" I shouted to Sanjay, and he complied. Hanover was up but I did not know whether he could run, so I scooped him up in my arms and ran as well. Justin, thinking it was a game, ran with us. We got to the gate of the dog run, and locked it behind us. A good thing, too, because the pit bulls had recovered their senses, and were close behind us. I looked back and saw the woman still sitting there, calm as can be, and holding tightly the leash of yet a third pit bull, much bigger than the others, with a muzzle on his mouth. If he had been let loose, Hanover and Sanjay and I would have been goners.

In the car, I called the police from my cell phone as Sanjay held the traumatized Hanover.

"We don't cover dogfights," the voice on the phone said.

"It was no dogfight. These two crazy dogs attacked my innocent dog." I wondered if Hanover had provoked them by bullying them. "They tried to get at my grade-school-age son!"

"The dogs attacked your son?"

"They tried to but we got away."

"I can't spare a car for dog-on-dog violence," he said. "If you want, you can come down to headquarters and file a report." I told him I would do that later. Right now, we had to get Hanover tended to. I looked at him. He was bloody but not bleeding profusely. I knew of a pet emergency clinic that was always open. I called them and explained the story.

"Bring him right in," the woman on the phone said.

At the clinic, Sanjay carried him in. They immediately took Hanover from his arms, and brought him into a room. We couldn't go in. I had to give them information about us, about the dog, and about the attack.

We sat in the huge waiting room for several hours. Fortunately Sanjay had a book in the car, and he was able to read for a while. He also walked up the road apiece. Nothing was happening today. It was Independence Day. I watched while other people brought in their pets. A cat which had been hit by a car. A dog with some skin condition which made him itch terribly.

Finally, they brought Hanover out. He was no longer bleeding, but he had a tube coming out of his neck. He was sleeping.

"He'll be all right," said the veterinarian. "He's lost a little blood, but not much. He just needs this tube in his neck to drain the fluid."

"Blood will be draining?" I asked.

"No, no. Fluid. He may have some pus, or some leakage. But he'll be fine. You should have the tube removed in a week. We can do it here, or more likely you'll want your own vet to remove it. I'll give you some pills for the pain."

Hanover was fine, thank God, and he was very chipper when the vet removed the tube. The vet scolded us for taking him to the clinic instead of his own practice,

"They charged you a fortune," said Dr. Boutrous. "I would have charged less than half because you're regular customers."

"But this was on the 4th of July. I was sure you'd be closed."

"For emergencies, we are always open. That very night we had an emergency to handle. Anyway, this dog is fine. I'll put stitches in him and come back next week to take out the stitches."

Hanover recovered, and soon he and Sanjay were back to their routine. As for me, the Yahoo group for the dog park had some ideas about the identity of the woman who owned the three pit bulls. I soon had her name and history which was not pretty, involving at least two other attacks on dogs at the park.

I found that the police actually had written up the attack, and so I got the police report. I filed a case in small claims court. On the day of our court appearance, we had to meet with an arbitrator, who would try to work out a compromise, before going in to court.

The woman refused to admit any wrongdoing. In fact, she denied being present at Watsessing Dog Park that day. But I had the police report. And. I had emails from the dog park group identifying her. Of course, the emails were not admissible in court, but she did not know that. We reached an agreement. She would pay half the $800 bill, in installments of $100 beginning next month.

The next month came and went without any payment. But as luck would have it, I was scheduled to testify as an "anti-character" witness against her in another dog attack case in Bloomfield. On entering, I spied her and went over to sit next to her as we awaited our case.

She apologized for not paying. "I lost my job. I can't find another and my unemployment checks are about to run out." I didn't know what to say. "Well, maybe you can pay just $70 a month?" She agreed. The case was postponed because the complainant did not show up.

But once again, no payment came.

At the next attempt to hear the case, I found her again. This time, in addition to an apology, she wrote out a check on the spot. I didn't know if it was good, but I accepted it. Her job situation had not improved. And there was something else.

"Today I have to go to the police and beg for my dogs back. They took them away from me. And they shot poor Remy. I hope he's all right. When the police came, he tried to protect me. He jumped on a cop and they shot him. I hope to God he's okay."

I did not tell her that I thought Remy would be put to sleep. She was shaking while talking to me. Once again, the complainant did not show up.

I never got any other payments, but decided to do nothing about it. I could have gone back to small claims court with a breach of arbitration, but I figured this woman had too many problems.

I did not want to be another one for her.

Hanover recovered well, and he and Sanjay went on together. It was several years later, and Hanover was (we thought) about twelve or thirteen years old, when his next adversity occurred. This one was not so easily conquered.

Sanjay and I were up at South Mountain Reservation, a wilderness area, with the two dogs, Justin and Hanover, we went on a short hike, but soon we lost the markings of the trail as we tried to keep up with the dogs, who were racing ahead. Finally, we grabbed the leashes and started to make our way out of the woods. The length of the hike was two miles, twice what we had intended. But when we got to the car, both dogs seemed in fine condition, and both leaped into the hatch.

That night at home we heard a strange, scraping sound coming from one room. Sanjay came to get Sharon and me.

"Hanover's scrabbling around," he said. "He can't get up."

There he was on the floor moving his forelegs, unable to move his hind legs.

We quickly put him in the car and headed for Dr. Boutrous. Though it was Sunday evening, we called ahead and found his Animal Hospital still open.

Boutrous scolded me for taking the dog on a long hike. It was supposed to be half as long.

"But he was fine, and he ran up the stairs when we got home," I said. Boutrous was unimpressed. He asked us to wait outside the examination room.

The office was full of patients. I guess few other places were open on Sunday evening. Shortly, Boutrous called us back in the room. Hanover had an IV going into him. "He has had a stroke," said Boutrous. "He can recover, but it will take time."

"And he'll be good as new, just like he was?" I asked.

"He'll never be just like he was. But he'll come back, to some extent."

Hanover was moved to a cage. He still could not stand. Sanjay stayed with him as I settled up the bill. To make Hanover a little more comfortable, Sanjay had brought one of his shirts from the hamper, so Hanover would get his scent. The dog lay on that shirt and looked forlorn.

Two days later, we were called back to the office. As we sat in the waiting room, we could hear Hanover's unmistakable mournful yelp. I asked the receptionist if he had been yelping continuously, and she replied, "No only since you've been here."

It was hearing Sanjay's voice which set him off. When he spoke again, out came the same yelp. Sanjay rushed back to see him while I asked the receptionist/nurse for permission. Of course, it was granted to spare the rest of the customers from that bone-chilling sound, and of course Sanjay was already at the cage.

Hanover quiesced when his master was near. I waited. After a long delay, Dr. Boutrous gave us some steroid pills and a natural brain enhancement herb, disconnected the IV, and there Hanover was walking again. I thanked him profusely and we were off.

At home, Hanover was relaxed, though he walked with his head tilted. He was able to go up and down stairs, and he ate, drank, and barked normally. But you could see something was different. In a few weeks, I got a refill of the steroids. Dr. Boutrous said that would be the last refill, the pills were not good for him long term.

In a few months, Hanover refused to go down the stairs. He was frightened. Going up was no problem for him, but there was no way he'd go down. So, Sanjay carried him down the stairs whenever he went down himself.

Then, in about a year, Hanover would not go up the stairs. He tried once or twice, but he always slipped down. Now Sanjay, in his senior year of high school, took to carrying Hanover up the stairs every night to sleep in his room, and down the stairs every morning for breakfast and to go out. Sanjay eschewed all extra-curricular activities (except Science League once a month, where he won major awards) so he could come home after school and spend the time with Hanover.

At this time, tragedy struck our family. Justin developed massive stomach bleeding. The vet stabilized him, but said it was just a matter of time. Justin passed away two weeks after Christmas.

Then one day, it happened. College. Sanjay hugged Hanover hard the day he left for college. I could see it was hard for him. Hanover, of course, did not know what was happening. Then his master was gone.

Now Hanover is home with us. He falls down a lot and makes messes frequently. But we try to be there for him. I carry him downstairs and feed him before going off to work, and carry him upstairs at night. Sharon carries him outside when nature calls. We will try our best with this dog, who has overcome so many adversities.

I Love My Pups
Lisa Scuderi-Burkimsher

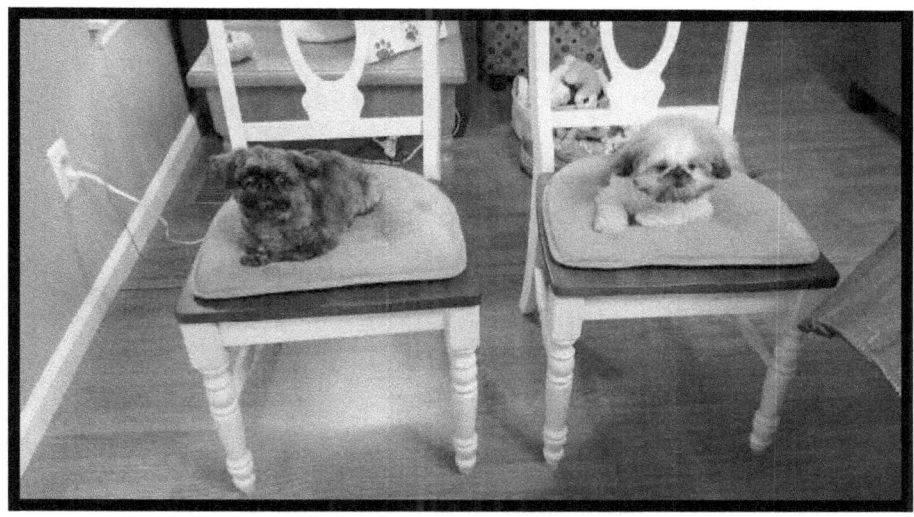

    Lucy Lu and Breanna Sue are both Shih-Tzu's. Although they're the same breed, each are unique in their own way, and I'm delighted they're my furry daughters.

    Lucy Lu loves playing with her favorite toy fox. She hugs it, trying desperately to get it to squeak. It's so old the squeak is gone, but it doesn't stop her from trying. She's a teacup and so tiny that when she sleeps in her bed, surrounded by all her toys, she looks like one of them. My favorite is how she loathes the dishwasher. She could be sound asleep, and when I open the dishwasher door very quietly to put a mug in, she'll jump up barking. She'll even stand in front of it for a while waiting to see if it goes on. When I do turn it on, she barks and barks until the quiet cycle comes on. It's these little things that make me love her even more.

    Breanna Sue is a puppy and a frisky one. She loves dragging our area rugs across the floor. Just the other day, I caught her dragging our decorative Santa across the room and chewing on his red coat. I saved it, just in time, before she chewed off a button. She's quick, too. When she's running, she makes me so tired, I must lay down afterwards. She absolutely adores Lucy Lu, but Lucy Lu doesn't care much for her puppy friskiness. One minute, she's running around the house, and the next she plops down exhausted. She even makes Lucy Lu tired. She's bigger than Lucy Lu, but Lucy Lu stands her ground and Breanna Sue just keeps playing with her. They bring so much joy to my husband and me, and it's wonderful to have them lay on our laps when we watch television, they're little bodies curled in a ball, content. They need us, and we need them more.

My life is joyful with Lucy Lu and Breanna Sue.

Keith's Dog
Mark Hudson

I remember taking art class twenty years ago with Mark Palmeri. He said I should stick to art techniques that work. He said I should break things down into groups of threes. Three sizes of paper, three sizes of canvases, limited palette of three, etc.

So, I did a painting of famous threesomes. I can't remember all the characters in the painting, but I think there was the characters from Rice Krispies, the people from Three's Company, the Three Stooges, etc. And then I put it all into one painting.

A friend, Keith, wanted to buy a painting of mine. So, I sold him the picture of threes.

Keith put the painting up in his kitchen. His dog took one look at it, and started barking furiously, like it was the weirdest thing he ever saw in his life.

And it was!

Lady
R. Bremner

Lady was simply the best dog I ever had. She had a calamitous life before we got her, but she was so sweet and happy and loved life so much she was an example to all of us.

It had been several years since our last dog, Samantha, and I had vowed never to have a dog again. But Sharon cajoled, begged, and bothered me so much, and she enlisted the aid of our son Sanjay to push and pull me toward a dog too.

I was determined not to get another Samantha-like dog. As much as we all loved her and as much as she loved us, she was vicious toward little children, and that I could not allow.

So, we made the rounds of the local shelters. In Hoboken, we found Companion Animal Placement, whose animals were fostered until permanent homes were found for them. The foster "parents" tended to keep several animals at once. There were a lot of homeless dogs. We were introduced to Jeffrey, who was part beagle and part something large, who was energetic and lots of fun to walk. My six-year-old son even took the leash for a short while. But there were a number of problems with Jeffrey. First, he had a problem with carsickness. Whenever he rode in a car, he would vomit. I suppose we could leave the window open, but then if he was bothered by cars, he probably wouldn't put his head anywhere near the window. The second problem was more serious. Being high-strung by nature, when something, anything made him nervous, Jeffrey would "nip". Which is another way of saying he would bite. Even his foster mother, whom he knew well and loved, had been "nipped" on several occasions. That was all we had to hear, with a vulnerable six-year-old at risk. So Jeffrey, cute as he was, was a no-no. We were told about another dog, but she was blind and very shy and they weren't sure that they could let her go.

The next stop was P.A.W.S., the Pound Animal Welfare Service in Montclair. They had a beautiful looking dog named Mountie. She was auburn-colored and seemed very calm when we walked her. I was almost ready to take her when a tall man with a cowboy hat strode into the shelter.

"I don't know if I'd recommend adopting Mountain," he said. "We don't know her history. She's only been here a week, and maybe her owner will show up looking for her. She might have just wandered off." I was about to leave our name and phone number when he continued, "Besides, we haven't seen yet how she relates to other dogs, and cats, and kids." We weren't going to adopt Mountie, or Mountain as the cowboy called her. It was plain to see his affection for the dog and his unwillingness to let her go.

A few days later, Sharon, my wife, informed me as I came home from work that we were going back to C.A.P. "There's Jeffrey. They want to convince us to take him. And there's another dog, a blind cocker spaniel whom Robin (C.A.P's main ambassador and a dog groomer by profession) promises I can see."

So back we came to C.A.P, who had no place of their own but worked out of the Hoboken Animal Hospital. Sanjay, my son, was glad to see Jeffrey again. Sharon went downstairs to see Robin at the grooming salon, where the blind cocker spaniel was. Sanjay and I visited with the dogs and cats upstairs at the clinic.

In a short while, Sharon called up the stairs to us. We joined her down below. And there, she held a fluffy, black dog in her arms. The dog was almost half her size and was shivering.

"The poor thing is frightened. See how she shivers," said Sharon.

"It's only because she doesn't know you," said Robin. "She's blind, and she doesn't know what's happening. She'll be better when she gets used to you."

"Pet her, Sanjay," Sharon said, and the boy reached ever so gently to her head. He stroked it softly. "This is Lady."

"I think we should take her," said Sharon. "She needs us."

I looked in Lady's face. You could not see into her eyes because a clump of hair covered them.

But as she moved her head and the hair fell away, I could see one glassy eye, and an empty hole where the other eye should be.

That night we talked about Lady. Robin had told Sharon her story. Lady was one of a number of cocker spaniels who were bred by a backyard breeder, a man who sold dogs for a sideline. But they were too closely interbred, and some health problems emerged. Lady's glaucoma was one of them, and her one eye could not see at all. As for the other eye, they didn't know how she came to lose it. Abuse was one possibility. Then there was a fire at the breeder's place. Lady was saved, and so were her "husband" and son. The puppy was sighted in both eyes. But the father had one bad eye. Like Lady, they could not tell if it was due to the fire or to physical abuse. He wore a patch and it looked quite jaunty. The breeder was prosecuted for his crimes, and C.A.P. took the dogs. The father and son, being purebred Cocker Spaniels and sighted (and Dad looking quite cavalier with his patch) were quickly adopted. But no one wanted Lady, blind, trembling Lady, with the weird looking eyes.

There was one other attempt to adopt her out. It was not a success. The home had another dog, and whenever Lady would misstep or bump her head, the other dog would bite her. The people returned Lady to Robin.

Sharon wanted her very badly. It was the maternal instinct, I think, and Sanjay talked about how we were getting three dogs: Mountie, Jeffrey, and Lady. So we decided on Lady, and I tried to explain to Sanjay that we weren't getting the other two. He smiled cheerfully and said, "Okay. Lady this week, Mountie next week, and then Jeffrey." I left it at that, not wanting to dampen his enthusiasm.

So, we brought her to our home. Lady was tentative at first, not sure of herself. But at least she stopped her shivering. I wondered how a blind dog would find her food, but it turned out we just had to fill her bowls of food and water, and she wandered over to them, albeit occasionally hitting her head on a chair or table leg. But she walked slowly and carefully, so she didn't hit her head so hard.

When we took her out to the backyard, she moved slowly at first. But then, as Sanjay and I stood on opposite ends of the yard, she would go from one of us to the other as each called to her, and as she began to grow in her trust of us, her pace picked up gradually until she was actually running in her strange plop-plop style.

Lady came to be very comfortable in our home, and she even learned a path to run to the front door and bark whenever anyone approached it. She was very happy in our backyard, and we even took her to the park on occasion, where she lost the fear of banging her head and let herself go.

After Lady had been in our home for several years, we "accidently" adopted another dog. We adopted him because he had run out of our house and got hit by a car, but he recovered nicely. Hanover fit into our home nicely and built a friendship with Lady. I think when we moved to another house, it helped both dogs that they had a companion to rely on.

The new house was much bigger. Our bedrooms were on the second floor, so the dogs came down with us to the first floor in the morning, and went upstairs with us at night. We thought it would be difficult for Lady, but she quickly learned to navigate the stairs, both up and down.

She was truly amazing.

After two years in the new house, we noticed a problem. Lady was huffing and puffing all the time, even when just lying down. We decided to take her to the vet.

Dr. Boutrous was an Egyptian doctor, a Coptic Christian whose home-office was always open. He loved animals and devoted his life to them.

"We're worried about her, doctor," I said, "Lady is about seven years old, and she's taken to wheezing."

"She's not seven years old," said the doctor. "Take it from me. Her teeth show her age. She's at least ten years old and probably older."

Dr. Boutrous took an x-ray. We waited for the results.

"Her heart is greatly enlarged," he said. "I'm sorry, but it's just a matter of time now. I can give you some pills to make it better, but they won't extend her life."

I was sorry that Sanjay had to hear that. His brow furrowed. He was thinking. "We'll go for another opinion," he said.

I agreed with him, who knows, maybe Boutrous was wrong. Sanjay was in school and me at work when Sharon took Lady to Dr. Brenda Queen, a highly regarded vet, who Sharon's friend had credited with saving her Sheltie's life.

Sharon called me at work.

"It's no use," she said. "Queen is even less optimistic than Boutrous."

"What can we tell Sanjay?"

"The truth."

We tried the truth, but Sanjay wouldn't believe it.

"Lady is okay," he assured me, sounding very mature. "She will survive."

And survive she did, for over a year, through several refills of the heart pills. Even more amazing than that, she insisted on navigating the stairs up and down. We tried to set her up both downstairs and upstairs so that there was no need for her to change levels, but she always crashed through the barriers to be wherever one of us was. Then one night it happened. I was working on my computer and Lady was sleeping in the hall, when my wife came in.

"Honey," she said in a quiet voice.

"What?" I asked her.

"Lady is not moving. She's not breathing."

I have had other dogs in my life before and after Lady, but never one so quietly loving as her. She was special. I was shaken. I could see that Sharon was, too.

The hardest thing, though, would be telling Sanjay. We decided it was best to be straight with him. "Lady has died," we said.

Sanjay was not buying it. "No, she's not," he said. "She just needs to go to the doctor." We could not convince him of her death.

There is an all-night emergency clinic several towns away. They take deceased dogs. Sharon wrapped a sheet around Lady and I gently lifted her into the hatchback of our station wagon. We left Hanover at home. He didn't seem to know what had happened. That was strange for such an intelligent dog. The three of us went with Lady in the car.

In the clinic parking lot, I lifted her out. She seemed remarkably light. Some poo had come out of her in the car. We didn't mind. Sharon said, "We're not coming in," and she hugged Lady goodbye. Sanjay said, "She's going to be all right. You'll see."

I carried her in. The girl at the desk told me to put her on a table in some room and come back. After I had finished with the paperwork, she asked me if I wanted time alone with Lady.

Alone in the room with the door shut, I said "Goodbye, Lady. You were the best dog ever. I love you." I hugged her. There was nothing more to say.

We were silent on the trip home.

Sanjay still believed that she was not dead. Whenever he asked about her, I would tell him, but he would say, "She's not dead, she's coming back to us. Why don't you call the doctor?"

Finally, Sharon and I adopted a story for Sanjay. Lady was on a worldwide tour with the doctor to help other blind dogs. She was now very famous, having conquered a heart attack and blindness, too.

Sanjay bought it. Each month he asked about her, and each month she was lecturing in another place. She was performing an important duty, teaching dogs around the world how to cope with being blind. One month, she was in France, the next month Japan, and so on. And when Lady's ashes arrived in the post, I had to hide them from my son.

Finally, after a year of this routine, Sanjay had had enough. "Lady's been gone too long. She's taught these other dogs enough. It's time for her to come home and be with us."

And then we sat him down and explained the truth. This time he was old enough to handle it.

So that weekend we gathered around in the far corner of the backyard, by our old black cherry tree. It was the three of us and Hanover, who gratefully was on his best somber behavior. We dug a hole, said a prayer, and commended Lady's ashes to the earth.

"Goodbye, Lady," said Sanjay. "I will never forget you."

Longing for Your True Home
Mark Hudson

My friend called at the last minute with a favor to ask, and I immediately put myself up to the task.

"I have to go to a hotel convention overnight, could you dog-sit my puppy so he'll be all right?"

"Yes," I responded to my good friend Ned, and began to clean up my humble homestead.

I didn't know if my apartment would comfort the pet, I thought it might be a place the creature would fret.

When Ned brought the dog, the dog began to whine, he didn't want to stay in that apartment of mine.

So lovingly dedicated to his master, so loyal, that there was no way I could make Levi feel royal.

Sometimes a dog can forget his master is gone, but Levi sniffed for his scent on all the lawns.

I must've taken him for eight walks around the hood, and for the most part, Levi behaved pretty good.

But being a puppy, he really enjoyed chewing, and it was something I tried to prevent him from doing.

But he would sink his teeth into certain items, chew them, play with them, and bite them.

I gave him a treat, in a corner he put it to hide, I'll keep it there to remind me of the puppy I tried.

It was an experiment, to see if a dog was a pet I could keep, and one thing I noticed was I did not get much sleep.

I walked him at four and six in the morning, in the dark, he saw someone's dog, and he was tempted to bark.

He also made friends with the neighborhood canines, he gently introduced himself and sniffed their behinds.

Towards the end, he laid waiting for Ned by the door, I hosted him in my home, but he could take no more.

He missed his master; I could totally tell it was true, he waited by the door, a puppy with a case of the blues.

Ned called, returning from stay at the hotel, and I took his puppy out of the place where I dwell.

When Ned got out of the car, Levi leaped in the air, so happy to his master, his joy was there to share.

There was a lesson to learn from the dog's attitude, about how having a home is a reason for gratitude.

As humans, we wish for more, never satisfied, but a dog just wants a human by its side.

Even though my apartment is mine and mine alone, I'm not some type of a king on a throne.

They say a man's home is his castle, but for some a pet is too much of a hassle.

I love women, children and the pets that exist, but my independence is a thing for which I insist!

One day of taking care of a puppy made me tired, so perhaps it's better that a dog I've not acquired!

But in my heart, I've adopted the creatures God made, and in my heart they will eternally never fade.

In heaven, they will bow with us before the throne, and I will personally give God's puppy a bone!

Lucky
Christopher Woods

    I knock softly, then slowly open the door. Teddy goes first, a short leash's length ahead of me. We enter another room for the dying. A man sleeps in one hospital bed, and in another, a woman is asleep. Single beds, I think to myself, and consider the irony. I take another step forward and see a woman, a sitter, in a chair around the corner nearest to the bed where the woman sleeps. The sitter is keeping watch for Mr. and Mrs. Carrington, an elderly married couple who are, unusually enough, in hospice together.

    Sometimes hospice patients hear us enter and wake. If they do, we make small talk. If they are able, they reach out to pet Teddy. He will then move closer to them, getting their scent, enjoying the attention. If they remain asleep, we linger for a moment, a kind of silent tribute perhaps, before making our exit.

    Teddy is a huge, completely white Great Pyrenees. He is also a therapy dog. My wife and I adopted him two years ago. He is four years old, and, as is often the case with rescue dogs, his earlier life was not the easiest. He was kept crated for many hours each day, so much so that his bottom teeth are pretty much gone. He kept gnawing on the crate door, but no one would let him out.

    Now he has a purpose. Great Pyrenees are often protectors of livestock. Sheep, goats, cows, horses and even geese are their charges. My wife Linda and I do not have livestock, so we decided to train Teddy to become a therapy dog. Pyrs like to have a job, and being a therapy dog seems to agree with Teddy.

    Neither Mr. nor Mrs. Carrington awakens. I make small talk with the sitter. I tell her that I remember the Carringtons from the year before, when they both lived in the Alzheimer's unit in this same retirement community between Austin and Houston, in rural Texas. We own a small farmhouse nearby. I remember that, when first seeing Teddy then, Mr. Carrington called to his wife Mary to come see the dog. Teddy is something of a spectacle, and this is not so unusual. But Mr. Carrington exclaimed, "The dog's tail is like a white bedsheet!" An odd visual description, but this is why I remembered this couple. On that day, Mrs. Carrington emerged from their room in the Alzheimer's unit to take a look. She smiled, apparently agreeing with her husband.

Now, Teddy and I leave the Carrington's' room, and I have the same thought I often do when visiting these people. I may not see them again. They will be gone. But I also know that someone else will soon take their places. There is a rhythm in this.

As Teddy and I walk down the hall toward another room, to the next person on my list, I think about the Carringtons. Death is a sad thing, yes, but there must be some kind of tender solace in departing life with your partner, your spouse, your husband or wife. Together. Such a strange thing, in fact, and I have not experienced such a thing before in any of our visits.

I look for my own wife, Linda, in the long hallway of disappearing lives. I do not see her, but I know she is with another person who also has a therapy dog. They are visiting someone else.

Alone with Teddy, I think about our own lives. We have been married over forty years, but there have been times when I doubted if we would continue. Six years ago, Linda was diagnosed with breast cancer. In addition to the surgery for that, it was also discovered that she had a thymoma, a tumor lodged between one lung and her heart. That required another surgery prior to the scheduled chemotherapy and radiation treatments. At the time, I had many doubts, as did Linda. What would happen next? What would become of us? But things worked out over the months that followed. Then, when Linda finished her last radiation treatment, I fell ill. I was so weak I was almost falling over. That was when I was diagnosed with colon cancer. Several operations later, I too began chemotherapy. Months later, I finished with it, and we both moved forward. Then, a year or so later, our beloved Golden retriever was diagnosed with lymphoma. River was gone in five weeks.

When we said goodbye to River, I think we were also saying goodbye to our personal cancer era. We decided to adopt a new dog, a different breed. We chose Teddy, and he has been a true blessing. A therapy dog, he takes us places we would never have ventured before.

I come to the next room, but before I knock softly on the door, I think of the Carringtons again. I think of Linda and me. How, on so many nights, we each watched the other suffer. We wondered what we would possibly do if the other departed early. I never considered how time and circumstances might change things, how we might depart together. The odds of this happening are very rare, indeed. So, in a way, I envy the Carringtons. Very few of us will be so lucky.

McKenzie
Carol S. Hanson

McKenzie came into our lives quite by chance. My older son, Eric, was seven at the time and his younger brother, Shawn, was five. Eric was just about to finish second grade and had a homework assignment that involved reading the newspaper and finding an article that he understood and could talk about. We had a rule at our house; snack, homework, free time. Back then, our newspaper was delivered by a paperboy. As soon as we heard that *thump* against the front door, we knew it had been delivered.

Eric was an avid reader, so I knew he could tackle this assignment fairly easily. He spread the newspaper out on the floor, and the next thing I knew, he was studying the classified section. There, he spotted a picture of a puppy that was for sale just a couple of miles from our house. We had not had a pet before, but we figured why not go over and have a look.

The dog was a miniature Schnauzer named Ozzie. *Ozzie???* If we purchased that dog, the first thing we would do is come up with a new name. Ozzie was already seven weeks old and ready to be weaned from his mother. We went outside for a little confab, and when we went back inside, we were the owners of a new puppy! Just like that!

I had always had a dog growing up, and I thought the kids were old enough to be responsible and caring for a dog. We decided that each of us would write down some names that we liked and then when I read the names aloud, there would be a vote. *Yea or Nay!*

There was some groaning and laughing at some of the names, but ultimately, we decided unanimously on McKenzie. We took McKenzie to the pet store with us so we could pick out some food and toys. We also purchased a crate, a collar, and a leash. We loaded all of the items in the trunk, and then I remembered we hadn't gotten him a food dish. Back into the store we went; got the dog bowl and a few other items, like a pillow for his crate. I could see the dollars adding up. Even though I had been a *wee bit* impulsive in buying a puppy, we were in for the long haul.

Next on my agenda was to sign McKenzie up for some dog obedience classes. That went well, and he passed with flying colors. I would take McKenzie for a walk almost every day. He was such a good walker. He knew to stay by my side, and he kept his sniffing and leg lifting to a minimum. Kids in the neighborhood would want to pet him while we were out walking. McKenzie was very obliging.

We also thought McKenzie was very athletic because he played basketball. I know what you're thinking, but it was our version of the game. We would get a laundry basket out, and McKenzie would promptly put his ball in it! *Tada!* Basketball! He also loved the game we called *Bally Wally down the Hally!* When we went to the lake, he would swim, and not just the dog paddle!

Even though McKenzie was as good as gold, he could create some random mischief. He wasn't a big chewer, but one day he got a hold of my Donna Summer album *On the Radio – Greatest Hits I and II* and chewed the cover. Fortunately, one record was on the record player, and the other was in its sleeve and didn't get harmed, so I took responsibility for leaving it on the floor. Thank goodness for vinyl!

Another time, I was going out for the day with a friend. When I returned, nothing looked amiss. The kids came home from school shortly after. Shawn had asked where the Fudge Jumbles were that I had made the night before. They should have been on the counter, but they were nowhere in sight. Hmm… we had a mystery on our hands. We looked around a bit and then I saw little pieces of tin foil spread around a living room chair. I looked behind the chair, and there to my surprise were the remnants of what was once a pan of Fudge Jumbles. McKenzie had climbed up on the chair and gotten the pan off the kitchen counter! Yikes!

The kids were upset because they were looking forward to their afternoon treat. But then the bigger realization came to us that McKenzie had eaten chocolate. We knew that could have terrible consequences. I couldn't tell how much he had ingested because of the mess he had made. I called the veterinarian, and she said to just watch him closely for a couple of hours.

We sat down to dinner that evening (minus dessert) and were enjoying our meal when McKenzie came over the table and without any warning threw up. Whew! We knew we were out of the woods, but did he have to gross us out at the dinner table??? It was *grotty to the maximum power!* A total *gag me with a spoon* moment!

Every Christmas we would get McKenzie a latex ball. We would wrap it, and he would sniff it out and proceed to open it. That was always a fun memory. He was the most accommodating dog. He didn't mind wearing a Christmas sweater or a birthday hat on his special day (well at least for a picture or two!)

When McKenzie was two, we had him neutered. Eric summed it up best with an analogy. He said, "McKenzie still had his suitcase; he just no longer had his socks." Out of the mouths of babes!

We also had a lot of nicknames for McKenzie. *Keezie Weezie* (said in a very shrill voice) and *Wacky Macky,* which came about after the chocolate incident. Sometimes I would sing "Little McKenzie, he's in a frenzy" when he would race around the house like a setter chasing a rabbit. As you can see, it was all about *rhyme time!* These names were all said with utmost affection. He was just the easiest dog to be around. I feel blessed that we had him for thirteen years.

Oh, and about that homework assignment that led us to McKenzie? That did get done, of course!

Mighty Levi
Mark Hudson

My friend Ned lost a dog over the summer,
a sad time, surely it was a bummer.
Emptiness embraced his solitude,
he got a new dog from a new brood.
He found a new puppy at the Wisconsin fair;
he and his daughter named him with care.
He was named "Levi" by his daughter Sophie,
the puppy himself was like winning a trophy.
My friend Ned was waiting to get employment,
so we took Levi to the beach for enjoyment.
Two of my friends that summer were out of work,
they're both employed now, wearing a smirk.
But they were available to hang out in summer 2016,
now I miss the camaraderie of the summer scene.
Going to the beach with the dog and his owner,
now it's almost winter, I'm now a loner.
But today is Black Friday, I saw a teacher friend,
off from work, for the Thanksgiving weekend.
So, there are always people to entertain my lonesome self,
maybe I need a dog myself, to keep my mental health.
My friend today talked about the creatures who share her home,
cats that climb on things and go from room to room to roam.
At first her husband didn't want cats, but he had to adapt,
now he loves them, and his wife must've just clapped.
How we love our pets, dogs, cats, and exotics,
a pet might prevent one from being psychotic.
I might need a dog, as my friends can come and go,
my sister has a dog-sitting and foster care business-Oh!
She has tried to encourage me to adopt a dog for board,
but I have too many possessions that I hoard.
But as I think of it now, a feeling of sadness appears,
I'm missing a dog of whom I could scratch its ears.

Am I fearful of the unbelievable expenses?
When approached to own a dog, am I on defenses?
Right now, my sister watches four dogs this weekend,
Thanksgiving weekend and four puppies sneaked in.
One of the puppies she is taking is "Mighty Levi,"
a puppy as brave as soldiers who fight and die.
At the doggie beach, he stood up to big mutts,
wrestled with them and almost kicked their butts.
But he was just playing; he knew when to quit,
at the doggie beach; Levi was a big hit!

New Lessons
Larry Lefkowitz

The lessons he had learned later were not the same as earlier ones—to fetch a stick, to roll over and wait for a hand to rub his belly, to beg. The later lessons were more complicated: to bark if he smelled that odor of leather; to refrain from barking when his master put a hand firmly on his neck—again when the men of leather were nearby; when attacking these men to part them from the long sticks they carried, from which came noise and fire that tore the flesh. To pounce before a leather man could raise the stick, before the fire could leap out. To leap for the hand that held it until it fell to the ground and his master or his friends killed him with their long sticks that made noise and fire, or the short sharp metal stick the length of the sticks he used to fetch.

He had learned to do with less food since he was not fed as well as before, more gristle and bone than meat, and this smaller, on the small creatures that ran in the forest. He had learned it was necessary to catch these creatures himself; sometimes he was allowed to eat them, sometimes the master took them and gave him a part. He was now a hunter, yet he wasn't allowed to wander far; if he smelled the leather men he knew to immediately return to tell his master, but first to lose the leather men if they followed him, easy since they were slowed by heavy boots. He did not understand at first why his master did not want him to kill and bring back a leather man as he did with the small forest creatures. It was his master and his men who searched for them in order to kill them. He did not understand this until something inside him like the odor from a long time ago, from his wolf past, told him that the successful pack surprised the hunted before it could escape or turn upon them. Because of this, he no longer thought of the leather men as men like his master, but as something less than human, as prey. Now when they dropped their sticks, he went for their throats, as did his ancestors. Now, like his master, he hunted the leather men as if they were the creatures of the forest.

He missed the former days when the master or others in the house of his master or the houses nearby would pet him and give him food, and he could retrieve the stick for the children and rollover and be petted. Now the master did not live in a house, but in the forest. Nor could he sleep as before, in his master's bed, near his warm body, or on the floor by the fire. Now he was often awakened, and the group moved quickly through the forest, and far off he would smell the smell of the leather men.

Sometimes they met children and the men gave them food and took them to a house outside of the forest and left them there; they were not like the former children; they looked fearfully at him and did not pet him. The few children that stayed with the group were like men, not children; they did not pet him when he rolled over nor laugh when he rubbed against their legs, only looked at him with sad eyes from which warmth had fled.

Even the animals like himself were no longer the same. A few moments before, for the first time, he had to kill such a creature held on a leather rope by a leather man when it went to attack one of the master's men. They had come to the edge of the forest where in the distance a great fence closed in buildings from where there reached his nose the smell of many people and another smell, stronger yet sweeter, the smell of the smoke which came from the sticks bigger than the men carried, higher than the trees of the forest, but he could not see the fire that he smelled. He had to struggle not to bark at the strange smells and the big fence, his master's hand firmly on his neck. And then another smell came to him, of animals like himself, like the creature he had killed, and something else. The odor of his ancestors again, this time closer; and the knowledge that these animals had been trained to attack men as he had once been trained to fetch a stick and roll over. The growl in his throat died at the tightened hand of his master.

The master and the other men waited; and then fire erupted with a great noise at a point in the fence and he smelled the odor of men coming closer, and more distant, of the leather men. Then the master's men ran toward them, and fire came from sticks of the master's men, and the smell of the leather men was replaced by that of the red substance. But the men that met with the master's men looked like bones, not men, yet with the shape of men, and he wanted to bite them because they were not men, but bones, although they walked like men. But the master quieted him, and the bone-men looked at him with fear, even after the master petted him to show them he would not harm them.

And all of them ran deeper into the forest.

He wanted to sleep for longer than the brief sleeps he was allowed, but the master and the other men did not stop walking for many days, unless it was to dig a hole and bury one of the bone men.

From far off came the smell of the leather men.

In the days that followed the smell of the leather men came closer.

One night their smell was very close and seemed to come from all sides as if the trees of the forest had turned into leather men, and suddenly many leather men ran at them, with the animals like himself, and there was much fire from the sticks, and his master fell, and the rest of the men and he leaped at the leather men and from the sticks fire came. This time the fire reached him; he felt it hot in many places, and he smelled the smell of his own red substance which mixed with the smell of the leather men, and he was afraid. He wished to lie down next to the warm body of his master, but his legs would not move, and the howl he wanted to shriek died in his throat.

Spice
R. Bremner

Spice was a simple dog. Not simple dumb, simple as in "plain and simple". She was easy to please. All she wanted in her day was to eat, drink, and lie down on a warm, comfortable bed.

Spice came to us one winter's night in a van with her five puppies. A rescue group had gotten her from a "kill shelter", one in which they give dogs a maximum of few days to stay. If they are not claimed by someone, they are put to death.

So, we agreed with the rescue group to foster the six dogs until the puppies were old enough to be adopted. That meant about two weeks, as they were already a week old. The gal from the rescue society, Jennifer, gave us two crates for the pups and mother.

Spice was a plain dog, with lots of soft fur, white and orange, who looked facially like a muskrat or badger. I wondered if she was a mutant mix with one of those. Later, we found that she was a likely mix of corgi (hence the thick soft fur) and beagle. Her face was singularly unattractive. She frowned steadily.

Spice was a terrific mother. She did something that I've never seen before, and am afraid to describe it here, for fear of disgusting all the readers. But she did it. And despite the puppy food which Jennifer provided to us, the pups were constantly at Spice's breasts. They were after her so much that she yelped in pain and started to run away. But then I swear she sighed as she gave it up and fell back into her motherly duties.

Fortunately for her, the puppies were eager to eat the moist food Jennifer had left for them and soon enough they abandoned their mother. Meanwhile, Sanjay took on the task of naming them.

There was Snowfly, the runt of the litter, who was the most aggressive when it came to eating.

Stormwind and Koochie were the philosophers of the group who could take food or leave it. Frederika was the largest and fullest and bowled the others over at mealtimes. Only Snowfly stood up to her.

Finally, there was Justin, named for my son's best friend who moved far away. There will be more about Justin in his own story, but for now, we can say that Justin, the only male of the litter and the biggest besides Frederika, was the shyest and retiring at the "dinner table", and he whined about it continuously.

Spice did not like to leave her babies for long. She was house-trained and very good at holding herself until we could get her outside. With a basement full of dogs, that was quite an accomplishment. She was very conscientious about it. She did her business quickly outside so that she could return to her little ones.

The one time that was trouble was when Sanjay picked up Justin to cuddle him. Spice jumped down off the chair to which she had retreated, and snapped at my son. She made a very ugly face and growled at him.

That was enough for Sharon. She rapped the dog on the snout and scolded her viciously. "Don't you dare snap at my son! Your days here are numbered, Missy! As soon as these pups are gone, you're gone!"

One day when they were old enough, we packed all the pups into a big cardboard box and drove them to an adoption clinic at Petco. Spice looked truly stricken when her pups were taken from her. She moped and put her head down. Sharon petted her and talked gently with her, woman to woman.

"We can't keep all of the puppies here," Sharon explained to her. "But Justin will live here. We're going to get good homes for all of them. They'll be very happy."

Spice did not look any happier. She looked most forlorn.

They all slept on the trip except for Justin, who whined so much that Sanjay had to take him out of the box and hold him on his lap.

It was a highly successful trip. Four of the puppies were adopted by nice people and families, and not only that, Jennifer made them promise to keep the names Sanjay had given them. "I just love those names!" she said. The only questionable one was Frederika, whose new owner wanted to call her Molly. We don't know how that one turned out.

We decided to adopt Justin ourselves. He was the puppy that Sanjay chose. A bond had been forged between them. I think that his constant whining made a special impression on Sanjay. When he held Justin, the pup did not cry.

But back home, Spice was not happy. When we arrived, she picked her head up looking hopefully, but her hopes were dashed. She continued to mope for several days. We asked Jennifer when she would come for Spice. She said that in a few days, a couple out in the country would be adopting her. "They keep asking me about 'our dog'!" she said.

But Spice had a definite problem. When she pooped, I could see little white things in her waste. None of her puppies had shown that. So we called Jennifer, hoping they had a vet who could help. Instead, she told us to take her to a local vet and the rescue organization would pay the tab.

The first thing the Katz and Dogz Animal Hospital did was to hydrate her. They put an IV in her neck and water flowed into her. They also gave her a treatment for worms, which was what I was seeing in her poo. We had to leave her for several hours while the hydration continued. They took a picture of Spice and Sanjay for their records.

When we came back, Spice had a huge smile on her face and a lump on her neck that looked like a tumor. Apparently, that was from the hydration, and would gradually go down. "And she's going to pee a lot." We were to bring her back in a few days for another deworming treatment.

Dr. Katzenbaum explained it to us. "These adult worms she's got are very tough to kill. And we can't do it all at once because it's too toxic for Spice. It will take three treatments."

"And then she'll be okay?"

"No, that's only for the adult worms. The babies and those not hatched yet are not killed. For them there are pills."

I wish she hadn't talked about "babies". It made me squeamish.

But it was as she said. Two more treatments, after each of which Spice was very happy (I think the hydration had almost a boozy effect on her), then pills to give her every day, and then after two weeks, she was clear. No little white things in her bowel movements.

But the cost of the treatments and the pills was getting expensive. And I couldn't get in touch with Jennifer suddenly. She wouldn't return our calls left on her answering machine.

Meanwhile Spice was settling in. She almost seemed to realize that she was not wanted, and she tried her best not to do anything that would aggravate us. She didn't bark at all, consumed her food and drink as soon as it was served, and did her duty outside and quickly returned to the house, where she lay down unobtrusively. I had to remark to Sharon that "She's doing everything right," to which Sharon agreed, "She's trying very hard."

Spice favored her left hind leg, occasionally holding it up while she limped on the other three. Jennifer had told us that Spice was found wandering the streets when picked up by Animal Control (new euphemism for dogcatcher), and so we thought her limp may have come from being hit by a car. And also, we thought that she must have been put out by her owner once she became pregnant. But it was all speculation.

Finally, we caught Jennifer on the phone. She said she had been out of state rescuing more dogs. Apparently, there had been trouble with the Spice's prospective owners. The old man had fallen and broken something and we'd have to keep Spice for a while longer. I assumed it was quite a while longer.

"Actually, we don't have to keep her at all," I said. "We can bring her to a shelter." Sharon started to object (Spice had conquered Sharon's early dislike of her, and she felt quite defensive about her now), when Jennifer said "Oh no, don't do that. I'm sure we'll be able to find her a home."

And the already $1,100 we had spent on her medical treatments? "I'm working on that."

To make a long story longer, the rescue group never made restitution to us and they decided to leave Spice with us. We were stiffed. We had no legal recourse because there was nothing in writing saying they would pay, or that Spice was not ours. They really couldn't care less if we brought Spice to a shelter but they bet that we wouldn't.

I was of two minds about it. I thought Spice was a really nice dog, but I felt that we couldn't really handle three dogs. There was Justin the puppy and Hanover the adult. Sharon had wanted to adopt Justin because she thought that Hanover might die in a year or two.

But now there were three. And Spice would have to be spayed soon, because we couldn't deal with another litter of puppies.

For the time being, we had Spice sleep with Justin in a crate in the basement. Justin would pass the night, but around six o'clock in the morning he would wake up and start to whine. Then Spice would bark because her baby was unhappy. We took turns in running to the basement and letting them out, carrying Justin quickly outside to house train him, and then walking Spice, who waited her turn patiently.

After a week, we retired the crate and let the dogs sleep in our room. Spice, despite her weak leg, managed to climb on the bed to relax, and it was impossible to get her off. In time, we grew quite fond of her and her soft fur. Neither of the other dogs was quite as soft. As Sanjay remarked, "Spice was made for human pleasure."

But her fur created another problem. Both Sharon and I became sniffly and sneezy because she shed so much. Finally, we decided to bring her to a grooming salon which advertised a "furminator" treatment, which not only dealt with the top layer of fur, but went underneath and handled the "undercoating" or so they said. I was skeptical, but Sharon wanted to give it a try.

We left Spice with the salon and received an angry call a few hours later. We heard a lot of loud barking of many dog voices in the background.

"You didn't tell us she wasn't spayed!" an angry voice said. "Don't you know 'it's the season'? All these male dogs are going berserk, jumping up in their cages and howling!"

They had finished her treatment, and I picked her up in that temple of cacophony. When she was home, we found that the furminator didn't do much good. She still dropped as much fur as before. However, we learned that with regular combings we could control the situation pretty well, and we could live with that.

Now that we had accepted Spice as a member of the family (she had already made herself a member all on her own), the next step was to license and spay her. At her spaying, the vet recommended glucosamine for her gimpy leg. We gave it a try.

The other two dogs much enjoyed going to dog parks and running with the other dogs. Not Spice. At the Lyndhurst dog park and the Watsessing Off-Leash Facility, her reaction was the same. She would jump up on the bench where I was sitting and bury her head in my lap, while Sanjay ran around with the other dogs. Every once in a while, some dog would make the mistake of trying to make friends with her, or poke its head at her. She would turn her face into an awful, ugly thing and growl and snap at the offender. The other dog would scamper away. Spice would then smile sweetly and go back to her resting in my lap. We only brought Spice to a dog park those two times. After that, we let her relax at home while we brought our other dogs.

So Spice became a dog of leisure, heading to a bed or futon whenever she could. And she ate, and ate, and ate. It was the life I guess she always wanted. Her gimpy leg improved remarkably. I don't know whether it was the glucosamine tablets or just the passage of time, but we totally forgot about the problem and were able to stop the tablets.

But another, more serious problem replaced the leg problem. After a few years, we noticed something odd. Spice would bump into things and seemed to have a hard time navigating her way around. She always moved slowly, but now she moved extra slowly. A look into her eyes confirmed it. She was not seeing us.

We spoke with the vet. I wish I could say that we immediately cleared her visual problems, but the condition was incurable. Progressive Retinal Atrophy, or PVA. There was nothing that could be done. Spice would be healthy in every other way, well-fed and loved and cherished, but she would be blind.

So that is where we are today. Spice is a wonderful dog, and she has learned to climb the stairs up and down quite easily. She just does it slowly. She has all she wants to drink and eat. She doesn't go out much, except for the necessary, but then she never did. She follows Sharon wherever she is, whether it's lying under her computer hutch or snuggled in the kitchen while dinner is prepared, or at night curling up comfortably in bed. She always has a big smile on a face that we now consider very pretty.

And she has all our love.

Sugar: Saying Goodbye
Audra Coleman

My dog died yesterday.

Last morning, I found her standing at the back door with a heaviness I had never seen before. She looked so, so tired... her head hanging low. We both knew. That very same night I had dreamt she was attacked by lions, and while I was desperately trying to save her life by stitching her together, a dear friend of mine appeared in the dream. She gently scolded me. "She chose to go in this way. Respect her choice." I don't know what the lions symbolized; maybe I don't need to know. I understood the message. So, I opened the door.

But that is where our journey together ended.

It was thirteen years ago when she became my dog and I her human. My dad had rescued her off of death row in a pound in rural Missouri on a hunch that she and I would be a "fit". Evidently, as a young puppy her previous owner had been an older woman who managed a pretty seedy trailer park on the rougher side of town. She had given the dog to her young granddaughter who named her Magentler, some kind of variant originating from "my gentle" dog. The woman had cited and fined several of the residents for letting their dogs run wild around the park. Well, as it turns out, the young "Magentler" was pretty adept at jumping fences and the formerly persecuted residents weren't going to stand for that kind of hypocrisy. She was forced to give the dog up.

When my dad gave her to me she wasn't quite one year old. She was a mix of Chow, Shar Pei, and a little "stranger in the night". Even though she was black, I named her Sugar. For the first several weeks, I had been asking her what she wanted her name to be. While waiting, I had defaulted to calling her Sugar, as kind of an interim nickname. When I asked her for the last time and she looked at me like I might be slightly obtuse, I finally realized that was the name she wanted all along... and so it was.

Oh my! When she was young all it would take was one playful sidewise glance and a slight feint forward from me and she would rip roar around corners of the house, fly over the back of the couch and throw her big old booty up in the air before throwing herself to the floor with a thud and a good roll on her back, all four paws flying every which way.

Years ago, my own mom admonished me that I needed to have a baby, a real *human* baby when I told her I had missed her call because Sugar and I were playing hide and seek. That dog travelled all over the United States in the back of a Jeep and later a VW. She chased squirrels with the spirit of Artemis, finally catching one and bringing it back to me. She suffered a pretty nasty gash on her nose as the squirrel did not "go gently into the good night". She was bleeding and panting heavily, but God was she proud. She was also pretty pleased with herself that every day for thirteen years she had kept those persistent intruders we call United Postal workers from approaching any further than our mailbox. She had done her job.

Children stepped on her, babies pinched her, maintenance men came and went, but I never saw her show her teeth except twice. In her early years, we lived in a first-floor apartment in Indianapolis. I was lying in bed when in the early hours I heard a bark from her that was distinctly different from any bark I had ever heard her emit. When I came to investigate, a clearly intoxicated man was attempting to crawl in the window and there was brave Sugar, keeping him at bay until the man fled as I called the police. The only other time was when I was walking her in downtown Asheville, and while waiting for traffic to cross the street, a man reached down to pet her. I didn't know the man, but her judgment was impeccable and good enough for me. I figure both times she may have literally saved my life or at least prevented some traumatic event from occurring.

I could fill a notebook with the memories we made together. She was smart, intuitive and compassionate, but most impressive was her spirit. She had HEART, the heart of a lion. But it was more than just memories. She never left my side, both literally and figuratively. She was always a step behind me, room to room, inside-outside. She slept with me or beside me every night and a shut door was not going to deter her. I had quite the argument with a passionate French man I dated over whether or not a dog belonged in the bed. A year ago, I moved my bed downstairs to the living room as it was obvious her arthritis was making the climb up the stairs to the bedroom an arduous one. But she made it clear, she was going to sleep beside me, even if she had to climb and descend those stairs every day. She was so tuned into me that I could wake up in the morning and open my eyes without making a sound and she would eerily sit up at the exact moment and look at me as if to say, "Good Morning, Friend." I could be in another room and start to silently cry and within minutes she would be pushing the door open staring at me with those compassionate eyes wanting to sit beside me until I pulled it together. She was never too busy, too tired, too anything to be distracted from her love and devotion to me.

But perhaps her greatest act of compassion came in her last year of life. Last year, I became pregnant and as it turned out, I would go through the pregnancy on my own. I felt alone, humbled and afraid in many ways. She was twelve and for a big dog that is pretty old, but I am certain she stayed around to see me through. On March 27th, I delivered a healthy baby girl. She greeted the baby with the same tenderness she had always showed me, but it seemed that in those three days I had spent in the hospital, she had aged another five years. Even still, she wasn't going to leave me until I had found my groove with the baby, until she was sure I was okay. In these last weeks, I would stroke her head after the baby was asleep and thank her, telling her she had done her job and that she had done it well. She had seen me through. She could go on if she was ready.

All these years I had imagined myself as her mother, but truth be told, she was mothering me all along. She offered me unconditional love. She loved me when my heart was broken and I was too depressed to get out of bed. She loved me when I was too busy or too preoccupied with life to take her on the walk I know she craved. She forgave me instantly a thousand times. She was teaching me how to be a good mother.

After I opened the door, I phoned a friend who rushed over to watch the baby so I might sit beside my other girl. I found her nestled on the edge of the garden lying next to a sprawling pink rose bush in full bloom. It was drizzling lightly. She liked the rain. She was still breathing, although labored. I sat beside her, petting her lightly. I thanked her again and told her it was okay. I was okay. And in her last breath, we let go of each other. She died a good death.

It has only been a day. Her bowls are still in the kitchen, her milk bones in the jar and her new bed lying on the floor beside the Diaper Genie. I still think she is right behind me. I still think I can call her name and she will find me. I can still feel her put her head in my lap. I don't know when all that will stop. I don't know if I even want it to stop. People say it was just a dog; I don't know what they mean. She was my most devoted and loving companion of thirteen years. In all my thirty-nine years, she is the best friend I have ever had, animal or human. She was family. She was my family.

Taking Care of Levi Part Two
Mark Hudson

It was Sunday, the day before the holiday for King,
and once again, my friend had his dog Levi to bring.
Since it worked out so well, the first time, so he claims,
he hopes I can dog-sit once a month, one of his aims.
Ned has a once-a month appointment at a hotel,
so I must take this puppy into the apartment where I dwell.
So he brought the puppy over, and this time Levi
was not so anxious, and well, neither was I!
He seemed a little bit more familiar with this "other" home,
but he would always sniff the leash, wanting to roam.
It started pouring rain, and the rain and snow was ice,
but that didn't stop Levi, he wanted out more than twice!
He found a blue ball lying perched in the muddy ground,
so for a half 'n' hour, he chewed the ball, like a hound.
People would walk by, with no umbrella, but I was still,
standing under a tree, feeling the cold winter chill.
It was worth it all for Levi, to watch him for the day,
to comfort and care for him, while his master was away.
Now my dad's wife has a sister, who got a new dog Willow,
my dad and wife Jane sit the dog, but he doesn't get the pillow.
Like father and son? Could it be? It sounds hard to comprehend!
My dad letting a puppy in, and considering it a friend?
It is his new wife Jane, that gave him that soft spot in his heart,
He'd better do what his wife says, if he wants to be smart.
Taking care of a dog twenty-four hours is harder than some know,
but dog-sitting is a way to get your puppy fix, even in the snow!
It means you get some exercise, and you have no excuse,
the dog will lead the way, and you'll just be his caboose!
You must keep his eye open that he doesn't scare the frightened,
if he fought with a dog, it would be "Clash of the Titans!"
Levi likes to play and wrestle, but he's a lovable pup,
when I take care of him, my spirits are always up!

The Guard's Dog
R. Bremner

The Toyota pulled up to the gate of the truckyard, and beeped its horn twice. An old man walked slowly toward the gate from the inside. The truckyard was only a short distance from the Pulaski Skyway, but might as well have been miles away from anything human. For in this desolate industrial park in swampy East Kearny, few things human were present to break the monotony.

The old man opened the gate. The guard did not know who the man was, but assumed that he was part of the family, or a friend of the family, that owned the truckyard. The guard parked his car by the side of the small office building. The old man grunted hello, as he did every Friday at three forty-five in the afternoon when the guard arrived to begin his shift. The guard always arrived promptly at fifteen minutes before his shift started, so he had time to change into his uniform. He went into the building and the interior of the two tiny rooms, which consisted of two lockers and a small bench. He took off his clothes slowly and methodically, and put on the blue uniform while the old man waited in the adjoining room. The guard did not come dressed, because he did not want his parents to know that he was a guard. They would have worried for his safety, so all they knew was that he was a fulltime college student. They had no idea how he spent his weekends, and the fact that he was out Friday and Saturday nights, well, they thought that was normal for a young adult male.

The now officially-dressed guard opened the door to the adjoining room and stepped into it. He asked the old man if anyone was in the yard. "Just some owner-operators. They'll be out of here before ya know it. It's Friday night, ya know." And with that, the old man was off.

The guard stood in the doorway, looking out at the four men standing around a truck cab, some fifty yards away. They did not appear to be working. With them was what appeared to be a small dog, lying in a relaxed fashion.

It was time for the guard's first rounds. He was required to make them every sixty minutes, carrying a clock that he would bring to each station, where he would find a key to turn inside the clock. He began his walk to the five guard posts that ran along the barrier fence. The second post brought him not so far from the men. He walked over to join them, with his notebook in hand.

"Hi, how're you doing?" he asked them. "Do you mind just giving me your names? Got to put them in the guard's log."

"Sure, why not," said the tallest of the men, who wore a shirt with all the buttons undone. "Long John Silver," he said, pointing with his thumb to himself. The nodding his head, said, "and that's Robinson Crusoe. Those guys over there," he indicated two shorter men in tee shirts, one of whom held a Coke bottle, "are Friday and Thursday."

"Really now," said the guard, trying to show amusement rather than frustration.

"Come on, Henry," said the second man. "Okay, I'm Tom O'Shea, he's my brother Henry O'Shea, and these fellas are Juan and Santo."

"Thanks." He scribbled the names in his notebook. "You guys going to be here awhile?"

"No way. We're wrapping it up now. It's the weekend."

The guard went back to his rounds, and he noticed that he had company. The dog was following him. "Hey!" he yelled, "is this your dog?"

"No!" came the answer. "That's some mealy mutt."

The guard noticed that the dog had no collar.

He was a little worried as he walked to the next station. This dog, with one ear flopped down in front and carrying the dust of the world upon him, might well be dangerous. The guard did not know dogs. His only experience was with a dog named Rex, whom he owned for two days as a fifth grader. His failure to walk or pay attention to Rex resulted in his father returning the dog to the pet shop.

But unlike Rex, who was impeccably groomed, this dog was a walking monument to filth. And how did the guard know what diseases he might carry? He didn't think the dog was rabid, but what else might be wrong with him?

The guard reached the second station, turned the key located there on a chain, and turned to the dog. "Look," he said, "I've got no food." He held out his arms to show the dog. The dog eyed him quizzically, and smiled with a mouth that showed several broken teeth. The guard worried that if not given food, sooner or later the dog would attack him. But for now, the dog followed along cheerfully, or so the guard thought as he completed his rounds.

The guard returned to the little office. He pulled the dilapidated folding chair outside, for it was less hot than the steamy building. When it would start to get dark, he would have to move inside for whatever small protection it would offer against the mosquitos who would visit in the evening. As he sat, the dog came to his feet and sat, looking up at his new friend. The guard didn't know what to make of this. If the dog got too hungry, the guard was sure it would fling itself at him in fury.

The two sat together in this manner for the next forty minutes, until it was time for the guard's next round. By now, the guard had come to notice that what he had thought were streaks of color on the dog's fur were actually streaks of dirt, and that his left ear was mangled, possibly chewed in a fight. The dog tagged along merrily as the guard walked to his first station. As he rounded the corner and headed to station number two, he passed the men, who had hosed themselves off and were now toweling themselves dry. He nodded at them. Station number three was at the far end of the yard behind some truck cabs, and out of visual range of the truckers. After this station, he could see two cars waiting to go out the gate and heard them beeping their horns. He ran to the gate, his keys jangling on his belt and the dog running along with him. He opened the gate, waved them through, and he was alone for the evening. The dog barked as the car left.

"Well, it's just you and me now, pal," he said to the dog. The dog was panting from his brisk run, and for some reason barked at the guard. "I don't have any food," the guard said in an irritated fashion. "I told you that." He finished his rounds with his companion at his side.

Things went peacefully enough for the next two rounds. The guard would sit and read, and the dog would sit very near him, as near as the guard would allow him to come. At the conclusion of his fourth rounds, the guard moved his chair inside, as darkness was falling and the mosquitos began to make their presence felt. The guard let the dog enter the building before closing the door. It would be hotter with the door and the one window to the place closed, but at least he could keep the mosquito population down. Somehow however, a few of them managed to get in, and he spent much of his time swatting them away. The dog merely sat contentedly. "Hey, you know you really stink!" said the guard. "Can't you sit over there?" The dog, however, did not move.

After his fifth rounds, the guard said, "You know, I was stupid. I should have used the hose on you. I bet you'd enjoy being clean." The guard thought a moment. "Come on, let's do it now. You'll like it." He walked swiftly over to a hose, which was hooked up to a spigot on the outer wall. He turned on the water, and the dog ran swiftly toward it. The slow flow of water quickly beaded on the dusty ground, and the dog, unable to drink, was confused as he ran around and around.

"Here," said the guard, "come here." He aimed the hose at the dog, but the creature leapt back. No matter how the guard coaxed, he could not induce the dog to let the water hit him. "Don't you want to get clean?" cried the exasperated guard.

An idea occurred to him. He slowed the flow of water even more, and held the hose with nozzle pointed upward. The dog, reassured, approached the flowing water and drank. The guard let him drink for several minutes, feeling sorry for the thirsty animal. Then all at once the guard gripped the dog by the fur on the back of his neck, and turned the hose on him. The dog struggled to get away, but the guard held firm, and despite his fears, the dog did not try to bite or claw.

There was no soap, but the guard managed to clean the dog with his hands. At first, the water running off the animal was dark grey. Within a few minutes it had turned to light grey and finally clear. The guard let go of the dog, which started shaking itself furiously. Eventually the shaking subsided, though every few minutes he would do it again. But he did not leave the guard's side and more than a little water hit the guard when the dog shook himself.

"There," said the guard. "Now doesn't that feel better?" The dog looked skeptical, but he seemed to enjoy the guard's attention, and came even closer to him. "Let's go back inside. The bugs are buzzing."

After his next rounds, it was time to eat his lunch. The guard unwrapped his huge sandwich of chicken, cheese, and mayo on an Italian roll. He took a bite. "Man, that's heaven," he said.

As he chewed, he was aware of the dog eyeing him hungrily. He thought he could even see the saliva on the corners of the dog's mouth.

"I guess you want something to eat," said the guard. "Didn't anybody feed you today?" Looking at the eager creature, the guard knew in his heart that none of the truckers, and certainly not the old man, had given the dog any food. With his fingers, he pulled out some of the chicken and held it out to the dog. The creature gently took it from the guard's hand, not snapping at it the way the guard expected. Once in his mouth, the food was instantly gobbled down. He stared quizzically at his benefactor.

"I guess you want more, huh?" he said. "I can spare a little more." Once again, he held chicken out to the dog, and once again the dog took it gently but then gobbled it quickly. "Oh heck," the guard said, and proceeded to tear up his sandwich and feed it in pieces to the animal. Chicken, cheese. bread, all were given over until the sandwich was completely gone. "Oh well. I wasn't so hungry anyway. I could certainly afford to cut back on my eating," the guard said.

So, the guard and his dog passed the night. The guard was indeed starting to think of the animal as "my dog".

Morning came. At eight o'clock, his double shift would be over. But no one came at first. The guard was dressed in his street clothes, ready to go home. The dog continued to shadow him. The day guard had to show up soon, or the night guard would have to do his first round for him. That was standard procedure.

At seven minutes after eight, the relief guard came. He was in a mood to chat, but the night guard wanted to get out of there. He started to leave then turned back for a moment.

"Goodbye, dog," he said. "I'll see you in eight hours."

****

At four o'clock in the afternoon, the banged-up green Toyota returned to the truckyard. The car stopped at the gate, and its driver beeped. Inside the gate, a nattily dressed young man left the side of his own car, a gleaming, still-wet Datsun, and walked to the gate.

The young man had a big smile on his face. He wore a short-sleeved gold Polo shirt which showed off his rippling muscles.

"Hello," said the newcomer. "I'll take it from here. You can go home." He looked around, but couldn't see what his eyes searched for.

"Okay, said the other. "Just let me finish wiping down my car."

"You washed your car?"

"I do it every week. Gives me something to do, and I don't have to pay for my own water."

Just then, a small dog came running out from behind the truck cabs.

"Hey," said the new guard. "Did you hear my voice? Good dog!"

"Yeah, that one's been hanging around. Had to chase him away with a stick, so's he wouldn't bother me no more."

"Oh. Well, me and him are old friends. We get along. Did you feed him anything?"

"Hell no. Why should I feed him? He ain't *my* dog. I chased him away when I ate my lunch because he looked at me hungry. Probably has disease or something."

In short order, the prior guard finished with his car and drove off. The new guard changed clothes and began his first round.

All alone now, the guard felt uninhibited in speaking to the dog.

"Wait till you see what I've brought you. I stopped at the supermarket on my way here. You're going to love it."

When his rounds were complete, the guard went to his car and extracted a grocery bag.

"Look at this! Cold cuts!"

He opened a sealed plastic container of roast beef and held a piece out for the dog to take. The dog snapped it up instantly, and it was gone just as fast.

"You like that, eh? There's more." And he peeled off a second piece of meat for the animal. Same result.

"You can have the beef now," said the guard, "but I'll save the turkey for later. I don't want you getting sick from eating too much. Or too fast."

The dog gobbled up what he was given. When the guard stopped parceling out roast beef, the dog lay down on his side with his full belly resting on the ground, and panting. I wonder when the last time was that he had a full belly, thought the guard.

It soon was time for another round. The guard embarked on his trip, with the dog prancing along, practically cavorting.

"Happy, are we?" the guard said. "I guess you've never had anybody pay attention to you before."

During the long, boring hours to follow, the guard sat outside and read. It was too hot to remain in the sweaty building. He tried to position his chair where he had the most shade, but such was difficult if not impossible. He also worried about the dog, who would not leave his side despite the heat. *It must be even hotter for him, with his fur coat*, thought the guard. Finally, the guard moved his chair to the space between two trucks, where there was some shade, and thankfully the dog went with him.

By nine o'clock, the sun was very low in the sky. The lights in the truckyard had come on, though this was the last round that the guard did not need them. The dog padded along. The guard did not feel so alone with his little pal going with him.

By nine-thirty, they had moved inside, for the limited protection against mosquitos.

And so, the night progressed. And went on to the wee hours of the morning. They had established a routine, walking the tours together. At three-thirty in the morning, the guard opened his second package of cold cuts, and fed the dog before eating his own lunch. Again, the dog ate eagerly and furiously, until his belly was filled, and he lay on his side, sated.

"Enjoy it while you can, dog," said the guard. "Who knows when there'll be more." Then sadly, he added, "Maybe never."

The next hours seemed to fly by. After his six-thirty tour, the guard said, "You know, you need a name. You can't just be dog." He thought for a while. "You're my buddy. So, your name will be Buddy."

And then came the seven-thirty tour, the last. The guard suddenly felt a rush of sadness. He spoke to his friend.

"I wish I could take you with me. But I can't"

Buddy looked up at him, smiling.

"I live with my parents and there's no way I can take you home with me." The guard wondered about that, but it was easier for him to reach that conclusion. "But I expect you to be here next week when I come, right?" But he doubted that as soon as he said it.

The dog's expression did not change.

And so, eight o'clock came and it was time to leave. The guard told his relief man to take good care of the dog, but the relief seemed not to take his entreaties seriously.

The guard stood at his car, about to get in. The dog was at his side.

"You take care of yourself, you hear? I want to see you next week when I'm back."

And with that he got into the car and drove off, not looking back. He knew that the dog would likely not be there next week. He knew that he probably could have begged and cajoled his parents into letting him keep the dog. But was the dog housebroken? What an embarrassment if he went in the house. No, it was easier this way. He felt like a heel. But he drove on.

He had gone almost two miles when he suddenly stopped. Fortunately, there was no other traffic on Fish House Road. He wheeled his car into a U-turn. He simply had to go back.

Arriving back at the truckyard, the dog, ignored by the other guard, seemed to notice his car. He made yipping noises as the other guard advanced to the gate.

"Forget something?" he asked.

"Sure did," he said, and as the other guard opened the gate, the dog ran through it into the arms of his master. The master picked up his dog and placed him gently in the back seat.

The Little Old Man and Pepi
Madelyn Kamen

It was a little, old man, stooped over a yellow wooden cane and walking a rust-colored Papillion, who happened by us that day. He was wearing an orange and red checked tam, topped by a red pompom, and baggy beige pants held up by green suspenders.

We were seated at a picnic table in the park, not far from our house. The man's dog ran up to us seeing that we had six little puppies of our own. Pepi, as we found out was the dog's name, let out a stream of yaps at seeing some possible playmates. Two of our dogs just sat there, appearing to wonder what the rust-colored creature was that only looked like them because he had four legs. Our four other dogs joined the yap-fest.

Johnny, Pepi's master, came forward and tipped his hat to us.

"How you folks doing this fine day?" he asked.

My husband, the friendlier of our family, spoke first, "Just fine, old man. How about yourself?"

"Oh, I could be better. You know, my rheumatism gets to me on days like this."

He was talking about the cloudy and somewhat moisture-laden atmosphere that threatened to turn a beautiful day into a stay-inside jail.

"Well, would you care to join us for a while and share some lemonade and sugar cookies?" my husband asked.

The old man shook his head, wiped his neck with a handkerchief and answered, "Don't mind if I do."

He sat down across from us on the picnic bench, poured himself a plastic cup of the lemonade, and took one long swig of the stuff. He let out a sigh.

"Everything okay, sir?" we both asked.

"Just call me Johnny."

"Still, you look a little sad, Johnny," I followed up.

"You have a good eye for sadness," he admitted. "My wife and I use to come to this park with Pepi here, and also have lemonade. She passed away this spring and now it's just Pepi and me."

"You seem lonely," I remarked.

"Well, nothing's really changed except she's no longer is in my life. She's not there at breakfast to sit and read the newspaper together, or after breakfast to work in the garden with me, pruning roses. And she's not there at noon to make sandwiches to bring to this park. Or in the afternoon, to sit and watch movies while I take my daily nap."

He took another long swill from his lemonade.

"And since you asked, she's not there at night to give me a rubdown on my back where the rheumatism is."

Johnny stopped talking abruptly to call Pepi to his side. We could see his nose start to redden and his eyes water. He looked down at the ground.

"Maybe, we should try another topic," I said, my voice barely above a whisper.

"Aw, no. You didn't do anything wrong." He took out his handkerchief again and wiped his eyes. "In fact, I'll just be moseying along now. Looks like it is going to rain."

The old man picked up his yellow, wooden cane, took hold of Pepi's leash, and doffed his orange and red-checked tam.

"Thanks for the company," he said, and walked off into the distance, satisfied that he had finally been heard by someone.

Walter
Margaret Peterson

Our country home, far from neighbors, felt lonely and, although I did not admit it to my husband, Bruce, I was nervous there.

"Let's get a dog," I suggested.

"Sure, Hon. What kind do you want?"

I knew so little about dogs that I said, "A big one."

He laughed and went online to show me various breeds.

Overwhelmed by the variety, I could not decide so we went to the S.P.C.A.

There I fell in love with a golden-haired dog, a mix of Shepherd and Labrador. He had large, expressive eyes and a look that touched my heart.

"He's pleading with us to take him home," I said. Bruce agreed.

We adopted him that day.

He was easy to train, companionable and fit into our household as if he had always been there.

He moved with a graceful dignity despite his size and deserved a name with class. I chose Walter.

He had been with us for a year when, for the first time, he and I were the sole occupants of the house. Bruce was away for the weekend and when night came and I lay alone in our bedroom panicky thoughts plagued me. What if an intruder broke in while I slept? Fear clutched me in its relentless grasp. Perspiration soaked me.

The house was silent, and I could hear the low, snuffled breathing of Walter as he lay in his usual place on the floor near our bed, curled up in his padded quilt.

A strange shuffle caused my body to tense. What was that weird sound? I held my breath and strained to listen. The noise was repeated and continued for several seconds.

I inched my head up from the pillow and peered through the room's dimness.

The sight of a dark form paralyzed me with dread. I stared helplessly at it until I realized it was Walter. He had dragged his quilt to the bedroom door and lay against it. He had sensed my terror and wanted me to know he would protect me.

I lay back, relaxed and fell into a peaceful sleep because of the comfort Walter had given me.

The next night Walter was on guard again at the door, but when Bruce came back on Sunday evening, Walter returned to his regular spot.

I never knew what a treasure we would acquire when I said, "Let's get a dog."

When She Goes
Jessica Rigby

She always leaves for years at a time.

She always says, "I'll be back in a few hours," then she waltzes in years later all like, no big deal, I'm home now. I get so mad when she leaves and so happy when she comes back.

I can't help but jump up on her with joy.

She says "no" and "bad dog" when I do this. It makes me feel sad when she says these things. She also says these things when she finds the trash can knocked over in the kitchen but hey, you can't leave a guy for years and not expect him to try and scavenge for his own food. Does she expect me to starve to death?

Also, I get so bored when she isn't around to throw the ball or tug the rope. Even the box on the wall that is full of movement and sound when she sits in front of it is quiet and black when she is gone.

Sometimes I chew on the sofa for a little entertainment. As a last resort that might help with the starvation thing too. I figure I might as well get used to the taste now.

Right now, I am waiting and trying not to be "bad dog" but there is a ham bone in the garbage calling my name, and she might never come back anyway.

Who Is In Charge?
Mark Hudson

In Evanston where I live, there is this latest thing going on where dog owners feel entitled to bring their dogs into every single Evanston business.

As a dog lover, I don't mind, but there might be other people who take offense.

On Wednesday, I was at a Whole Foods, and a woman came in with her little white dog on a leash.

She was trying to pull the dog in one direction, and the dog was going in another direction.

So she would yank the leash, and the dog would go sliding across the cement floor on its paws.

Yesterday I was walking in downtown Evanston with my friend Chris, and we saw two people walking a bulldog, and the bulldog was leading the couple on the leash. My friend Chris said,

"Who is walking who?"

Dogs nowadays are like kids nowadays.

They're running the show! Think carefully before you buy a dog, or have a kid. Both are a worthwhile investment, full of love, but the price is expensive! And either way, be prepared to lose a lot of sleep!

Contributing Authors

Finnigan

A.J. Huffman's poetry, fiction, haiku, and photography have appeared in hundreds of national and international journals, including *Labletter, The James Dickey Review,* and *Offerta Speciale,* in which her work appeared in both English and Italian translation. She is also the founding editor of *Kind of a Hurricane Press.* www.kindofahurricanepress.com

Audra Coleman currently lives in West Asheville and is currently devoting her energy to enjoying and learning the art of mothering.

Bobbie Groth's stories have found homes in literary and horror magazines like *Mused, The Crime Factory, Rosebud, The Wagon, Tigershark,* and a Grey Wolfe Publishing's *Legends* anthology. She has signed a publishing agreement for her first historical novel. As a former expert witness in murder cases, Bobbie lightens her spirit by spending summers in a fishing village in Maine, playing Celtic fiddle, and keeping very large dogs next to her at all times. Follow Bobbie at

https://www.facebook.com/bobbie.groth.7
https://twitter.com/Gooseknoll
https://bobbiegroth.wordpress.com/

Carol Hanson

Christopher Woods is a writer, teacher and photographer who lives in Texas.

http://christopherwoods.zenfolio.com/

Jon Moray has been writing short stories for six years and his work has been published in several online and print markets. When not working and spending quality time with his family, he enjoys writing and playing sports.

Larry Lefkowitz's stories, poetry, and humor have been widely published in journals, anthologies, and online. Lefkowitz's literary novel, *The Novel, Kunzman, the Novel!* is available as an e-book and in print from Lulu.com and other distributors. Writers and readers with a deep interest in literature will especially enjoy the novel. His humorous fantasy and science fiction collection, *Laughing into the Fourth Dimension* is available in print from Amazon books.

Lisa Scuderi-Burkimsher was born and raised in Staten Island, New York.

She realized her love of writing comes from her love of reading. Several years back, she took online writing courses to hone her skill and is currently involved with an online writing critique group and a fiction book club. Her short flash *The Big Duke*, was published in September of 2015. She had several micro flash shorts published the same year, including *The Plunge*, and continues to have her work published. She has stories in the *Winter Writes* anthology, the *Halloween Musings and Amusings*, anthology, and Grey Wolfe's *Write to Woof 2016* anthology.

Lisa currently resides on Long Island, New York, with her husband Rick and little dog Lucy Lu.

Madelyn D. Kamen, PhD., is a freelance writer and the founder of a document development and consulting firm. She was an associate dean and professor at the University of Texas Health Science Center at Houston. She has published short stories, poems, and essays in local and national magazines and newspapers and online. She was a graduate of the Texas Leadership Class of 1992 and has been listed in *Who's Who In America In The Southwest* and *Who's Who In America*. Her collection of short stories, *Crazy Lady In The Mirror*, has been Published by Silver Boomer Books.

Mark Hudson is a prolific writer and has been a frequent contributor to *Legends, The Grey Wolfe Storybook, Write To Woof, Write To Meow* and other Grey Wolfe Publishing anthologies. He is currently working on a collection of short stories.

R. Bremner, of Glen Ridge via Lyndhurst, NJ, USA, is a former cab driver, truck unloader, security guard, computer programmer, and vice-president at Citibank. He writes of dead kings and many things he can't define, incense, peppermints, and the color of time. All things Beat, Dada, and surreal are his loves. Ron was in the very first issue of *Passaic Review*, along with Allen Ginsberg. He has appeared in *International Poetry Review, Oleander Review, Paterson Literary Review, Yellow Chair Review,* and *Poets Online* (20 times) and sundry elsewheres. Find his inexpensive books *You are once again the stranger, Poems for the Narrow,* and *Stories of Love and Hate* at Amazon, BN, Lulu, and Smashwords. Ron is a member of the *Montclair Write Group* and reads with the *Red Wheelbarrow Poets*.

Please visit him at *Poets & Writers:* http://www.pw.org/content/r_bremner , where milk and cookies await.

Wolf Haven International is a nationally recognized wolf sanctuary that has rescued and provided a lifetime home for 200 displaced, captive-born animals since 1982. Guided 50-minute walking visits offer guests a rare, close-up view of wolves. Wolf Haven provides a variety of educational programs, participates in multi-agency Species Survival Plan programs for critically endangered wolves and advocates for wolves in the wild.

www.WolfHaven.org

Wolf Haven International
3111 Offut Lake Rd. SE, Tenino, WA
360.264.4695 or 800.448.9653

www.ingramcontent.com/pod-product-compliance
Lightning Source LLC
Chambersburg PA
CBHW060815050426
42449CB00008B/1672